SECOND EDITION

Introduction to Play Analysis

CAL PRITNER

SCOTT WALTERS
University of North Carolina–Asheville

WAVELAND

PRESS, INC.
Long Grove, Illinois

For information about this book, contact:
Waveland Press, Inc.
4180 IL Route 83, Suite 101
Long Grove, IL 60047-9580
(847) 634-0081
info@waveland.com
www.waveland.com

Copyright © 2017 by Waveland Press, Inc.

10-digit ISBN 1-4786-3467-7
13-digit ISBN 978-1-4786-3467-6

All rights reserved. No part of this book may be reproduced, stored in a retrieval system, or transmitted in any form or by any means without permission in writing from the publisher.

Printed in the United States of America

7 6 5 4 3 2 1

*We dedicate this book
to our wives,
Evamarii Johnson and Laura Walters*

About the Authors

CAL PRITNER, PhD, chaired theatre departments at Illinois State University and the University of Missouri–Kansas City, and was the founding artistic director of the Illinois Shakespeare Festival. Pritner, an inductee of the College of Fellows of the American Theatre, was the co-author of an instructional television series on Shakespeare and on poetry, and co-authored *How To Speak Shakespeare*. In addition to his academic career, he acted on stage, in television, and in film, and he directed professionally in the theatre. He lived in New York City.

SCOTT WALTERS, PhD, is Professor of Drama at the University of North Carolina–Asheville, where he recently received the Award for Teaching Excellence in the Humanities. He has served as Assistant to the Dean of the College of Fine Arts at Illinois State University, as well as Associate Artistic Director of the Illinois Shakespeare Festival. He has written for *American Theatre Magazine,* the *Huffington Post,* and *The Clyde Fitch Report,* and founded the Center for Rural Arts Development and Leadership Education (CRADLE). He writes at Creative Insubordination (www.creativeinsubordination.com). He lives in Bakersville, North Carolina.

Contents

Preface xi
Acknowledgments xiii

Introduction: The Why and What of Play Analysis   1

Why Analyze a Play? 1
What Is Analysis? 2
Reading at Multiple Levels 2
The Glass Menagerie 5
The Influence of Aristotle, Stanislavsky, and Others 6

LEVEL ONE
First Impressions

1   The First Reading   11

Play Analysis Leads to "Doing" 11
Techniques for a First Reading 12
A Structural Concept of
  Comedy, Tragedy, and Drama 19
A First Reading of *The Glass Menagerie* 20
Questions for a First Reading of Any Play 21

LEVEL TWO
The Essence of Drama

2   Conflict 25
  Concepts in Conflict Analysis   26
  The Structure of Dramatic Conflict   27
  Process for Determining the Conflict   28
  Conflict in *The Glass Menagerie*   31
  Questions about the
    Conflict-Resolution Structure in Any Play   34

LEVEL THREE
Gathering Information

3   Given Circumstances   37
  Given Circumstances: Stated and Implied   37
  Accuracy and Given Circumstances   38
  Research Sources   39
  Backstory: Events and Relationships
    that Precede the Play   39
  Setting: The Play's When and Where   39
  Social Systems that Affect the Characters   40
  Cultural Norms   41
  Plays in Translation   43
  Plays in Fantastical Settings   43
  Plays Emphasize Different
    Given Circumstances   44
  Gathering Information on Given
    Circumstances in *The Glass Menagerie*   44
  Questions about Given Circumstances
    in Any Play   50
  Organizing Information about
    Given Circumstances   51

4 Theatrical Contract — 53
Contracts vs. Conventions 54
Presentational and Representational Contracts 54
Realistic and Nonrealistic Contracts 57
The Theatrical Contract in *The Glass Menagerie* 60
Questions about the Theatrical Contract in Any Play 62

LEVEL FOUR
Interpretation

5 Characters — 65
Aspects of Characters 65
Stage Directions as Character Information 69
Language Informs Us about Characters 69
Dialogue Suggests Characters' Physical Actions 71
Characters Evoke Conflict,
 and Conflict Reveals Character 72
Characters in *The Glass Menagerie* 73
Questions about Characters in Any Play 77

6 Conflict Analysis Applied to a Scene — 79
The Scene as a Unit of Conflict 79
Conflict Analysis Applied to Scene 2
 of *The Glass Menagerie* 80
Smaller Units: Actions and Beats 84
Actions and Beats in *The Glass Menagerie* 85
Questions on the Conflict-Resolution
 Structure in Any Scene 86

7 Supplemental Research — 87
Types of Supplemental Research 88
Summary 93

LEVEL FIVE
Bringing It Together

8   Synthesis — 97
   Conflict vs. Theme   97
   Relating Other Elements to Conflict   101
   Questions about Synthesis in *The Glass Menagerie*   105
   Questions about Synthesis in Any Play   107
   Testing and Enriching Our Analysis
      through Outside Resources   107
   Conclusion   107

Appendix 1: Analyzing Shakespeare's *Hamlet* — 109
   The Text of *Hamlet*   109
   The First Reading   110
   Given Circumstances   113
   Theatrical Contract   118
   Character, Language, and Thought Process   120
   Conflict Analysis   122
   Supplemental Research   123
   Synthesis   125
   How to Set *Hamlet*?   125

Appendix 2: Character Maps — 127

   Key Terms   131
   Index   133

Preface

The premise of this book is simple: We believe that to succeed in the theatre, students must have strong skills in analyzing plays. As theatre teachers and practitioners with decades of experience between us, we have seen over and over again artists with great talent, creativity, insight, and emotional depth fail to achieve success because they couldn't recognize how plays they were doing *worked*. Consequently, their considerable efforts ended up working against the fundamental power of the play with disastrous results. This book seeks to remedy this all too common situation.

We believe that no matter what point in your career—student, amateur, professional—you will find something in this book that will help you to strengthen your artistic choices and deepen your understanding.

Organization of the Book

We provide a step-by-step approach to play analysis. We take the reader through multiple levels of reading a play, beginning with the basic skills needed to get the most out of the first reading, continuing with identifying the conflict, gathering the play's "facts" and the interpretation of its events and characters, and ending with a synthesis of all of those elements into a unified whole. This approach progresses from a purely subjective and personal response, through the objective gathering of information, and on through higher and more complex levels of interpretation.

At the book's center is the premise that *conflict is the essence of drama*. Conflict is the engine that drives the play, and it must be finely tuned in order to run smoothly and powerfully. We believe that, at root, people attend the theatre in order to watch characters in conflict with each other and it is the artist's job to communicate that conflict with imagination, depth of feeling, and clarity.

Chapter Organization

Each chapter begins by introducing a concept that is then explored by studying its application to Tennessee Williams's *The Glass Menagerie*. We have chosen *The Glass Menagerie* as our model play because it is simultaneously accessible and complex, and it allows us to explore in a single play all of our analysis process. Occasional examples are also taken from Sophocles's *Antigone*, Molière's *Tartuffe*, August Wilson's *Joe Turner's Come and Gone*, and William Shakespeare's *Tragedy of Hamlet*. (Hamlet is also treated intensively in Appendix 1, which is about Shakespeare, his times, and special issues of analysis that his plays demand.)

Finally, each chapter ends with questions that can be applied to any play being analyzed.

Acknowledgments

Like most students, teachers, and artists, we've synthesized, translated, reinterpreted, and added to the ideas of others. We acknowledge our obvious debt to the genius of Aristotle and Stanislavsky. We have also been influenced by Kenneth Burke, whose considerations of dramatism revealed the centrality of conflict to the understanding of drama and theatre. We encountered Burke through our colleague John W. Kirk. We are also grateful to the students we have taught over the years, and the artists with whom we have collaborated. They have inspired and challenged us to deepen and clarify our ideas.

The following people, who read and commented on the manuscript in various stages of development, made important contributions to the final result:

    George W. Bellah III, Central Washington University
    Karen C. Blansfield, University of North Carolina at Chapel Hill
    Andrew Vorder Bruegge, St. Cloud State University
    James Buglewicz, East Los Angeles College
    John J. Conlon, University of Massachusetts, Boston
    Larry Dobbins, Missouri Western State College
    William A. Earl, Wartburg College
    Ira Hauptman, University of North Texas
    Marjorie Hayes, University of North Texas
    Valleri Robinson Hohman, University of Arizona
    Lin Holder, St. Cloud State University
    Kristin Johnsen-Neshati, George Mason University
    David W. Johnson, Virginia Polytechnic Institute and State University
    Michael E. King, Northern Kentucky University

Dennis M. Maher, University of Texas at Arlington
Thomas J. Manning, University of Wisconsin, Oshkosh
Jane T. Peterson, Montclair State University
Mark Pizzato, University of North Carolina at Charlotte
Mary J. Schuttler, University of Northern Colorado
D. Terry Williams, Western Michigan University

Introduction
The Why and What of Play Analysis

Why Analyze a Play?

We analyze because artistic play production involves more than merely reading a play and "putting it on its feet"; more than nominating a director who assigns roles to actors who speak the dialogue and follow the stage directions; more than the director and designers following the play's descriptions of costumes, scenery, lighting, and sound effects. To discover and communicate the potential of any play, especially a great one, involves more than simply reading the play as if it were a blueprint or a recipe to be followed step by step. Play texts demand more than following directions; they demand analysis and interpretation. By analysis we mean the process of identifying separate elements of the play, and by interpretation we mean the process of clarifying and communicating our understanding of the elements we identified. For purposes of simplicity and economy we refer to the overall process as play analysis.

We analyze plays because theatre is an art form with the potential for greatness, the potential to engage audiences and to enhance their understanding of what it is to be human. The creation of a great theatre production is a complex process involving many decisions and several artists. Play analysis guides us in the exploration of a play's complexities, helping us explore a great play's profundities and guiding us as theatre artists in the process of collaborating and communicating during the production process. Mere reading and staging may occasionally result in brilliance, but theatre artists cannot rely on the lucky accident.

We assume you are reading this book after some experience of the theatre. You know what theatre is. You probably have attended theatre and have read plays; you probably have some familiarity with what directors, designers, and actors do. Because you are studying play analysis, we assume you aspire to a higher level of engagement in theatre, seeking to ascend beyond mere reading and doing, aiming for involvement as a mindful, purposeful artist of the theatre. We focus here not on separate play analysis techniques for designers, for actors, or for directors; rather, we present a system of play analysis that applies to all theatre artists.

One of the most important aspects of play analysis within the context of the creation of a production is to provide the artists with a common vocabulary for discussing the play and for reaching agreements concerning how the play is to be realized on a stage. Without a set of common understandings, a production will lack coherence and unity—it will simply be a hodgepodge of competing visions.

What Is Analysis?

We have suggested part of the answer: **Play analysis** is purposeful, systematic, interpretative reading. It is a process of multiple readings, reading each time with specific purposes and asking increasingly complex questions about the text. Theatre artists synthesize the results of these close, interpretive readings into a new understanding of the play that is profoundly greater than could have been achieved by a surface reading.

Once you have analyzed a play, you are better prepared to design, rehearse, and perform with confidence in the knowledge that you understand the play's structure and meaning. Through this process you transform stage directions and dialogue into a comprehensive understanding of the written play.

Reading at Multiple Levels

Our central premise is that systematic, interpretive play reading leads to theatre productions that fully embody the potential embedded in the text of a play. Our approach to play analysis, which involves reading at multiple levels, consists of a sequence of play readings that build on one another. Each reading involves increasing levels of complexity, leading to a final synthesis that combines separate elements into a coherent whole. This series of readings involves analysis (identifying parts of the play), interpretation (clarifying our understanding of the parts), and synthesis (bringing the parts together into a coherently interpreted whole).

The process demands that you examine purposefully the play's separate elements. You must understand the components before you can synthesize them. You must examine how the story is told, when and where it is set, how the "when" and "where" affect the story's characters, how the characters interact with each other and with the audience, how they

Introduction

speak and think, how they agree and disagree, and how the playwright intends the information to be shared with the audience.

Because this is your introduction to play analysis, we make no assumptions about what plays you have read or seen. Instead of making references to a variety of plays, we have chosen one play, Tennessee Williams's *The Glass Menagerie*, as our model play for analysis in each chapter. We have chosen it as our model play because it is an exceptionally good play that is simultaneously accessible and complex. You may have encountered *The Glass Menagerie* before. If so, we hope you will put aside previous impressions and interpretations in order to experience fully and effectively this system of play analysis.

In addition to *The Glass Menagerie*, we occasionally use examples from four other plays: Sophocles's *Antigone*, Molière's *Tartuffe*, August Wilson's *Joe Turner's Come and Gone*, and William Shakespeare's *Tragedy of Hamlet*. *Hamlet* is also treated intensively in Appendix 1, which focuses on Shakespeare, his times, and special issues of analysis that his plays demand.

In Chapter 1 we suggest a process for your first reading of *The Glass Menagerie*. We have designed examples from the other plays in a manner that should illustrate our point even if you haven't read the complete play.

The First Level: First Impressions

Because first impressions are important, we introduce in Chapter 1 key techniques for the first reading of a play, including systematic note taking. The reader's first impressions come from two main sources—dialogue and stage directions—and note taking can help you to record these impressions. Also, we recommend recording your impressions of the play's overall mood.

The Second Level: The Essence of Drama

Conflict analysis begins after we have read the play and know how the plot's events transpired. Understanding the structure of the conflict opens the door to understanding all other aspects of the play: Conflict (Chapter 2) is the essence of drama. By this we mean that for an event on stage to be dramatic it must have conflict. To understand how the play happens, you must understand more than the story. You must comprehend the underlying conflict, for conflict drives the play. Our conflict analysis system asks, Which character drives the conflict? What forces oppose the central character? What moments in the conflict must be identified and highlighted in order to clarify the play's essence?

The Third Level: Gathering Information

Gathering information involves analyzing and interpreting details of time, place, and values (Chapter 3). These details are called the given circumstances, a term coined by the great Russian actor, director, and theorist Constantin Stanislavsky. Analyzing and interpreting given circumstances may be easier for plays set in our contemporary time and culture than for plays set in times, places, and cultures that differ from ours. Whatever the play's time and location, you must ask how factors such as politics, economics, religion, ethnicity, family, and cultural values affect the characters' thinking, their language, and their behavior. Many questions will arise as you read, some requiring research and all demanding analysis and interpretation.

Reading to gather information also involves asking what kind of relationship the play creates between the audience and the production (Chapter 4). Some plays create a contract in which characters acknowledge the audience's presence, frankly treating the audience as an audience, the theatre as a theatre. Others create a "fourth wall" between the characters and the audience, never acknowledging the audience's presence or recognizing that the play is taking place in a theatre. Furthermore, plays differ in the ways they use language, scenery, and costumes realistically and nonrealistically. You must analyze and interpret all of these elements.

The Fourth Level: Interpretation

When reading at the level of interpretation you focus first on characters (Chapter 5), raising questions of fact: What do the characters do and say? What do others say about them or do to them?

When reading at this level you also study how characters differ from each other. Great plays possess characters who are interesting because they are unique and complex: neither simply honest nor dishonest, neither always selfish nor unselfish. In other words they are situational. Like you, they behave differently according to circumstance and situation, treating their mothers differently from their siblings, using different language with their friends, their family, their teachers, and so on. Part of the interpretation and analysis of characters involves identifying and clarifying these situational aspects of character.

At this level you also analyze how characters are affected by their given circumstances. How do economics, religion, education, culture, and family affect one character differently from another? Your answers to these questions will fuel the way you individualize and differentiate characters.

In addition to introducing a systematic treatment of a play's central conflict, we also analyze an individual scene, studying how conflict analysis can be applied to moment-to-moment play analysis (Chapter 6). Why? Because analysis demands that you understand the play at every moment, and to understand any scene, or any moment, you must comprehend its essence, or its conflict.

After you have systematically analyzed a play, you may want to turn to outside resources (Chapter 7). There can be value in researching the playwright's background, the play's production history, and criticism of this play and others by the playwright, but this step should come after your own analysis, before being influenced by others.

The Fifth Level: Synthesis

Analysis of the play's parts (characters, ideas, themes) is interesting and informative, but your ultimate goal is to reach a comprehensive understanding of the play (Chapter 8). In reading for synthesis you reexamine the information gathered at each preceding level of analysis. You apply the supreme test of your understanding of the play by creating a narrative statement that synthesizes your analysis. The act of synthesizing your analysis into a written statement tests your ability to bring to bear all of the questions you've asked about the text.

Because conflict is the essence of drama, the conflict-resolution process functions as the play's core. Therefore, conflict analysis is the central tool you use in building a statement that synthesizes your analysis. Great plays present multiple themes that you must identify and celebrate. Likewise, great plays involve complex characters who deserve careful analysis. But, for themes and characters to be unified into a coherent interpretation, a framework must exist that holds them together. The conflict-resolution process is that framework around which themes, ideas, and characters are unified. Play analysts depend on the conflict-resolution process for this source of unity. A synthesis of the play must reflect and be congruent with the analysis of its conflict.

Is this process difficult? Yes. Will individuals arrive at differing analyses? Of course—indeed, the existence of differing interpretations is the mark of a good play. One of us recently came across old lecture notes for a play he was currently teaching and found that his earlier conflict analysis was entirely different than what he was currently teaching! Nevertheless, the process is a valuable one: it demands reading, analyzing, and interpreting at multiple levels, and it demands synthesizing the readings into a statement that weds the readings and the conflict analysis.

The Glass Menagerie

Each play has a unique form; therefore, analyzing *The Glass Menagerie* is a process special to the play that cannot be duplicated exactly when approaching another play. But the questions that we ask and the concepts we use in studying *The Glass Menagerie* will apply to other plays as well. Like a tennis match in which the same strokes are used in every game, but in a different order and in different circumstances, likewise, the concepts and questions of play analysis will be relevant to all plays, although the process of using them changes from play to play.

We have chosen *The Glass Menagerie* as our model play for multiple reasons. Among the most important reason is its complexity. Because of the play's richness and complexity, individual analysts will likely reach different conclusions about its very essence: its central conflict. We celebrate that paradox as being the evidence of a play's greatness. Nevertheless, we hasten to add that a multiplicity of ideas about a play does not mean that all analyses are equally valid and equally profound. Interpretation is not arbitrary, nor is it simply the result of personal taste and creativity. It is the result of careful consideration of all aspects of the text and the knowledge that comes from that consideration. The American director Zelda Fichandler says, "Imagination is what is there after you know everything; without knowledge, one's imagination may be too thin—lacking in strength and too fragile to build on."[1] Play analysis is not a substitute for imagination; it is a crucial precursor to imagination, the foundation upon which imagination stands. We present here a process of analysis that has the virtue of being systematic, a process that asks questions intended to stimulate perceptions through which artistic imagination can flourish.

The Influence of Aristotle, Stanislavsky, and Others

It may be said that Aristotle, a fourth-century B.C.E. Greek philosopher, is the forefather of play analysis. Aristotle lived and wrote after the period of the great Athenian tragic playwrights Aeschylus, Sophocles, and Euripides. In his *Poetics*, he contrasts theatre with epic poetry, justifies theatre as an art form, describes the nature of tragedy, and identifies and defines what he considers the central elements of playwriting and theatrical production. His categories, standards, and recommendations have influenced theatrical theorists since their rediscovery during the Italian Renaissance.

Aristotle's *Poetics* is important historically for his description of the six elements of drama: plot, character, thought, diction, music, and spectacle. Although this textbook uses terminology that differs from Aristotle's, our play analysis process is inspired by his effort to create a comprehensive and systematic approach to understanding plays.

Aristotle says that the most important element of a drama is its plot, by which he means the arrangement of the incidents or actions. Like Aristotle, we explore characters by studying their behavior (Chapter 5). Our central thesis regarding characters, influenced by Aristotle, is that characters are revealed by the way they treat others and by the way they respond to others' treatment of them. In other words, characters are defined by their actions.

Like Aristotle, we see plot as important to drama. But there are major differences: Aristotle explores plot as the arrangement of major incidents through which a play's protagonist progresses. We, however, center on conflict (Chapter 2), which we define as the struggle of the protagonist to overcome opposing forces. One might say that Aristotle's emphasis is on the incidents through which the protagonist struggles, whereas we focus on conflict (the protagonist's struggle to overcome opposing forces) as the central element of drama. Also, we identify a structure through which typical dramatic conflicts move from their inciting moment to their resolution.

In our study of conflict at the level of scenes (Chapter 6) we apply the study of conflict to a segment of a play, a scene that has a conflict with a beginning, a middle, and an end. In the scene chapter we use Aristotle's term *action*, but we use it in a way that is influenced by the ideas of Stanislavsky, whose ideas are useful in exploring moment-to-moment events through which a character moves. Stanislavsky and his followers use the terms *action* and *beats* in a manner that is influenced by and related to Aristotle's theories.

In Chapter 5 we address character in a way that includes Aristotle's concepts of thought (the process of exploring ideas and emotions) and diction (in his terminology, the arrangement of verse). We subsume these concepts by examining characters' use of language as revelatory of how they think and how they treat others. One might say that the chapter includes the influences of both Aristotle and Stanislavsky.

Aristotle's term *spectacle* addresses spectacular stage effects. Rather than studying scenery, costume, lighting, properties, and stage effects as elements of play analysis, we consider these elements to be topics directors and designers will consider after they have analyzed the play. Instead we concentrate on identifying and interpreting the theatrical contract (Chapter 4). As part of the contract, we ask, What relationship between audience and stage does the play create? And does the play treat its elements realistically, or does the play abstract such elements as time, character, and language?

NOTE

[1] Arthur Bartow, *The Director's Voice: Twenty-One Interviews* (New York: Theatre Communications Group, 1988), p. 111.

LEVEL ONE

First Impressions

1

The First Reading

In the Introduction, we described a play analysis process involving multiple, systematic levels of reading. Obviously the first reading is the first level, the time when you introduce yourself to the play.

Play reading is a special process, different from most reading such as of fiction, newspapers and magazines, or letters and e-mails. Play analysis involves a unique process of gathering information from the title, the stage directions, and the dialogue, all with the goal of imagining everything on the page taking place live before an audience.

Play Analysis Leads to "Doing"

In reading narrative fiction (novels or short stories), we read for enjoyment of story, character, the use of language, and the author's insights into the human experience. The greater our skill as readers, the more we absorb fiction's complexities, gathering and appreciating every intricacy the author has embedded in the work. But no matter how skilled our reading, we are not called upon to complete the novel by performing it, by "doing" it. Even literary critics read with the goal of thinking, writing, or speaking about the reading experience. Critics expect to write or speak about a piece of literature, but they don't expect to do it.

Of course, we can read plays in the same way we read fiction: for pleasure and insight, perhaps also to write or speak about the play. Play analysis, on the other hand, is a skill that leads beyond pleasure and insight to doing. In play analysis, we read for information that we must act upon, information that we will eventually physicalize as directors, designers, and actors. In one way or another we will embody the information on stage for an audience. Therefore, even in a play's first reading we must absorb information with a different kind of consciousness than narrative fiction demands.

Because you are reading plays to analyze them, you must undertake a first reading systematically, understanding that first readings provide impressions you want to retain, examine, and analyze. In this chapter we recommend specific techniques for the process.

As we noted in the introduction, we use a single play as a model for play analysis: Tennessee Williams's *The Glass Menagerie*. We recommend that you postpone reading or rereading it until we have introduced our techniques for the first reading.

Techniques for a First Reading

Read the Play in One Sitting

Most plays can be read in two to four hours. Because your first impressions of a play are so important, we recommend allowing time to read in one sitting. *The Glass Menagerie* can be read in two to three hours, but taking notes may add an hour or more to the process, so allow four hours for the first reading.

Why one sitting? For one thing, that's how a theatre audience will experience the play, as one evening of theatre. Part of analyzing a play is imagining an audience's first experience of it in the theatre. Subsequent analytical readings will demand that you focus on limited aspects of the play (for example, given circumstances, character, conflict). In the first reading, you are seeking to form a first impression of the play. You are asking yourself to absorb it as a whole, to perform multiple tasks simultaneously: keeping characters and their relationships in mind, reading descriptions of objects and persons and visualizing them happening in time and space, imagining the sounds and rhythms of human speech, and absorbing the play's emotions and moods. All this demands a special kind of concentration that can best be achieved by reading in an uninterrupted session.

Also, this will be the only time you encounter the play without knowing how it ends, so that each moment will contain the suspense and surprise that an audience will experience. Cherish this opportunity to experience something fresh!

Because we assign specific tasks for this first reading, we recommend you keep a pencil handy for writing in the margins of the play, noting items that will require attention later. Also, put a bookmark on the cast list page; for many plays, you'll find yourself returning to it frequently. Our model play, *The Glass Menagerie*, has only four characters, but many Shakespearean plays have two dozen, some of whom are referred to by multiple names.

Note Unfamiliar References and Words

Plays may be set in cultures or historical periods about which we know little, and they may use unfamiliar vocabularies. Note these unfamiliar references in the margins. Any item that is unfamiliar or confusing to you will likely be unfamiliar or confusing to an audience encountering it for the first time. Although this note taking slows your reading, it is best to note your questions and confusions while they are still fresh, before numerous readings have made it difficult to recall your experience of the first time. Later, especially when you are analyzing the play's given circumstances, it will be useful to refer to these marginal notes. We recommend that you not stop to look up these words and references during your first reading—simply note them and look them up later.

Visualize the Stage Directions

Stage directions, often printed in italics, represent suggestions regarding the play's setting, its sound or lighting effects, and perhaps the characters' appearance or behavior. In some editions of a play, the stage directions come from the author; in other editions they may be a mixture of the author's instructions and an editor's additions. Play leasing companies such as Samuel French Inc. and Dramatists Play Service publish acting editions that may mix the author's stage directions with directions from an editor (sometimes taken directly from the stage manager's promptbook for the original professional production). In some cases it is relatively easy to distinguish authorial directions from an editor's; for example, there is a scholarly tradition that in William Shakespeare's plays the stage directions taken from the original printing appear in italics and editors' directions appear in brackets. In other editions it may be more difficult to determine the origin of stage directions.

Until you become expert at determining the origin of stage directions, our advice is simple: read them. Later you may wish to compare editions of the play. For the first reading, use the stage directions, along with dialogue, as sources of valuable information. Assume that the playwright included them in the text because he or she felt the need to communicate information important for understanding the moment.

Plays differ substantially in the amount and kinds of information they provide through stage directions. For example, Shakespeare's plays contain few stage directions, usually indicating only entrances and exits, almost never providing stage directions that indicate where the scene is taking place. Some Shakespearean plays have no indications of act divisions.

On the other hand, modern playwrights often describe stage settings in detail. Some describe characters' appearances, and others even tell us about characters' emotional lives. In *Joe Turner's Come and Gone,* August Wilson tells us about time and place, proceeds to identify the interior (kitchen right and parlor left), then lays out the entrances and exits, and even tells us where the doors lead:

SETTING

August, 1911. A boardinghouse in Pittsburgh. At right is a kitchen. Two doors open on the kitchen. Two doors open off the kitchen. One leads to the outhouse and Seth's workshop. The other to Seth and Bertha's bedroom. At left is a parlor. The front door opens into the parlor, which gives access to the stairs leading to the upstairs rooms.

There is a small outside playing area.

This is a fairly traditional set description. Wilson proceeds immediately to tell us about the historical, cultural, and social background from which his characters come:

THE PLAY

It is August in Pittsburgh, 1911. The sun falls out of the heaven like a stone. The fires of the steel mill rage with a combined sense of industry and progress. Barges loaded with coal and iron trudge up the river to the mill towns that dot the Monongahela and return with fresh, hard, gleaming steel. The city flexes its muscles. Men throw countless bridges across the rivers, lay roads, and carve tunnels through the hills sprouting with houses.

From the deep and the near South the sons and daughters of newly freed African slaves wander into the city. Isolated, cut off from memory, having forgotten the names of the gods and only guessing at their faces, they arrive dazed and stunned, their hearts kicking in their chest with a song worth singing. They arrive carrying Bibles and guitars, their pockets lined with dust and fresh hope, marked men and women seeking to scrape from the narrow, crooked cobbles and the fiery blast of the coke furnace a way of bludgeoning and shaping the malleable parts of themselves into a new identity as free men of definite and sincere worth.

Foreigners in a strange land, they carry as part and parcel of their baggage a long line of separation and dispersement which informs their sensibilities and marks their conduct as they search for ways to reconnect, to reassemble, to give clear and luminous meaning to the song which is both a wail and a whelp of joy.

Some might call this long description a preface; others might call it a long stage direction. Obviously, most of this description will not find its way in any literal sense onto the stage of a production. Nevertheless, the characters in the play do arrive carrying bibles and guitars, do lay roads, and do try to find meaning in their own songs, and these stage directions serve to place those characters in a context, a social and historical milieu, which will shed light on their situation in the play. After having described the play's setting and context, Wilson begins describing the action:

ACT I

SCENE I

The lights come up on the kitchen. Bertha busies herself with breakfast preparations. Seth stands looking out the window at Bynum in the yard. Seth is in his early fifties. He has a stability that none of the other characters have. Bertha is five years his junior. Married for over twenty-five years, she has learned how to negotiate around Seth's apparent orneriness.

Later in the first act, Wilson introduces other forms of stage directions. First, a direction that combines an action (entering a door) with a character description:

Jeremy enters the front door. About twenty-five, he gives the impression that he has the world in his hand, that he can meet life's challenges head-on. He smiles a lot. He is a proficient guitar player, though his spirit has yet to be molded into song.

Another direction mixes a character's physical action with explanation of his behavior:

Seth stares at Loomis, sizing him up.

Part of the play analyst's responsibility in the first reading is to ask, If the playwright has provided this information through stage directions, what is its purpose? Is the information in the stage directions important for storytelling purposes? Or is the playwright supplying this information merely to affect my thinking about the characters?

Theatre artists must develop the habit of visualizing descriptions of settings, costumes, lights, sound, and characters that are supplied in the stage directions. A motto for first readings is, *If the script describes it, take the time to visualize it.* Because visualizing the set's floor plan is especially important, we recommend creating a diagram of the stage layout, including the locations of doors and major items of furniture.

Pay attention to descriptions of characters' physical actions. A single physical action may prove to be central to the play's plot. At the end of *Joe Turner's Come and Gone,* for instance, Loomis has just had a confrontation with his wife, during which he has taken out a knife and slashed his own chest and, as a result, has suddenly come to "a realization." Wilson writes, "Loomis turns and exits, the knife still in his hands. Mattie looks about the room and rushes out after him." The fact that Mattie, a woman to whom Loomis has been attracted but whom he has been unable to reach, is the one who follows Loomis, as opposed to his wife, Martha, is significant to understanding the transformation that has just occurred in his life. Without reading the italics, that important piece of information would have been missed. Despite the recommendation of some authorities, we believe it is important to read stage directions carefully. You can choose later to ignore some and accept others.

Gather Information from Dialogue

Reading **dialogue** requires a heightened awareness. The play analyst must read like a detective, always on the lookout for information that may turn out to be important. Read dialogue with the assumption that talk reveals essential information.

Often the dialogue gives specific information about where the play is set: What nation? State? City? Neighborhood? Whose home are we in? What is the season of the year? Time of day? Is climate important?

In the opening of Shakespeare's *Hamlet,* we learn in less than a dozen lines that it's dark, it's midnight, and Barnardo and Francisco are standing guard (our comments are in brackets):

Barnardo: Who's there?
[Barnardo can't see Francisco.]

Francisco: Nay, answer me: Stand and unfold yourself.
[Neither can Francisco see Barnardo.]

Barnardo: Long live the King.
[They serve under a king.]

Francisco: Barnardo?

Barnardo: He.
[By now they probably see each other.]

Francisco: You come most carefully upon your hour.
[He's on time.]

Barnardo: 'Tis now struck twelve, get thee to bed Francisco.
[It's midnight, bedtime.]

Francisco: For this relief *[relief from guard duty]* much thanks.
'Tis bitter cold, and I am sick at heart.
[Now we know the weather!]

Hamlet was written for an outdoor theater, at a time before stage lighting could indicate time of day. Shakespeare uses dialogue efficiently to communicate useful information.

In addition, we must study dialogue for cultural information: economic conditions, educational levels, religious affiliations, and ethnic prejudices. For example, along with Hamlet, we learn from the Ghost of his father that he's in Purgatory (Act I, Scene 5), which tells us that the play exists within the religious context of Catholicism:

> Ghost: I am thy father's spirit,
> Doom'd for a certain term to walk the night,
> And for the day confin'd to fast in fires,
> Till the foul crimes done in my days of nature
> Are burnt and purg'd away....

From dialogue we learn about the characters and their relationships: Who are the mother and father in this family? Who are the sons and daughters? The bosses and the laborers? The lovers? The opening scene of Molière's *Tartuffe* provides information about character relationships through dialogue. As the curtain rises, Madame Pernelle enters angrily, followed by Elmire, Mariane, Dorine, Damis, and Cléante. After a few lines, the following exchange occurs (we have italicized each bit of information concerning relationships):

> Madame Pernelle: ... *Children*, I take my leave much vexed in spirit.
> I offer good advice, but you won't hear it.
> You all break in and chatter on and on.
> It's like a madhouse with the keeper gone.
>
> Dorine: If ...
>
> Madame Pernelle: Girl, you talk too much, and I'm afraid
> You're far too saucy for *a lady's maid*.
> You push in everywhere and have your say.
>
> Damis: But ...
>
> Madame Pernelle: You, boy, grow more foolish every day,
> To think *my grandson* should be such a dunce!
> I've said it a hundred times if I've said it once,
> That if you keep the course on which you've started,
> You'll leave your worthy father broken-hearted.
>
> Mariane: I think ...
>
> Madame Pernelle: And *you, his sister*, seem so pure,
> So shy, so innocent, and so demure.
> But you know what they say about still waters.
> I pity parents with secretive daughters.
>
> Elmire: Now, *Mother* ...
>
> Madame Pernelle: And as for you, child, let me add
> That you behavior is extremely bad,
> A poor example for these children, too.
> *Their dear, dead mother* did far better than you.

	You're much too free with money, and I'm distressed
	To see you so elaborately dressed.
	When it's one's husband one aims to please,
	One has no need of costly fripperies.
Cléante:	Oh, Madam, really . . .
Madame Pernelle:	*You are her brother,* Sir,
	And I respect and love you; yet if I were
	My son, this lady's good and pious spouse,
	I wouldn't make you welcome in my house.

From the dialogue we learn who each character is and what their relation is to each other. In addition, the personality of each character has been described (although whether Madame Pernelle is a good judge of character remains to be seen).

By reading like a detective we learn what information characters share: the information that is the common knowledge of a community, a family, or a couple. And we must ferret out what information one character knows that another doesn't know. Shared and unshared information will affect the plot and character relationships.

Dialogue Is Doing

In play analysis we must think of talk as action: one person doing something to another or getting something from another. Dialogue reflects a character trying to affect her relationship to another, trying to get someone to behave differently.[1] This may involve the character trying to get someone to think more highly of her. Or it may involve the character getting the other character to perform a specific action: to do something, go somewhere, or say something. At any rate, we must learn in play analysis to think of dialogue as doing.

Dialogue Reveals Characters

Some plays describe characters' moods and motives through stage directions, but play analysis demands that we interpret **characters** more precisely than can be done in any but the most extensive stage directions. Play analysis requires that we "read" people through word choice, through analysis of the tactics that their words reveal. As you read for the first time, study how characters speak differently to others. For example, how does a character speak to her boss? To her boyfriend? To her mother? Father? Sister? How does her language reflect the fact that she uses different tactics (strategies for getting what she wants) in each of her relationships?

Later in our levels of reading we devote a chapter to analyzing character, but even in your first reading you can gather information about characters and their actions from their dialogue.

Be Aware of the Play's Mood

Does the play give you the impression of being serious or comic? Does it make you want to laugh because you feel superior to the characters' foolishness? Does it make you want to cry because you feel such sympathy for them? Whatever your reaction, try to understand what information made you react as you did to the play's **mood**.

We are not concerned in first readings with literary analysis of plays. We are not asking you to apply theories of tragedy or comedy. Instead, we are urging that you attempt to understand your own reactions to the play's overall moods. Ask yourself, What is my emotional response to the play? What prompted this response? How might an audience experience the play in performance?

Any subject can be the source of comedy: politics, illness, love and marriage. Just imagine the television situation comedies you have watched. Situation comedies depend on us seeing that characters are predictable and overcommitted to an outcome they seek, or overcommitted to a way of being seen by others.

Likewise, the same topics that can be treated comically can be treated as serious drama, even as tragedy. Again, the mood grows not out of the subject but out of the way the subject is treated.

The ability to read a dramatic situation on the page and to identify its intended mood is an important skill for play analysts. Some day you may be choosing to produce a play; ideally, your interpretation of its mood, the playwright's intended emotional response, will be critically important to the process of preparing a production for your audience.

The important skill is to detect the mood (comic, serious, tragic, or perhaps a mixture) that the playwright seems to be trying to create. You must use stage directions, dialogue, and your own sensitivity to determine, at least provisionally, the mood toward which the playwright was aiming. You may disagree with the playwright's intent, perhaps disagree with her decision about how to treat a subject dear to your heart, but you must develop your ability to interpret accurately the playwright's emotional intent and strategies. If you don't like what the playwright has done, that's a matter of preference; you may decide you dislike the play and may avoid seeing productions of it. The play analyst's necessary skill is to interpret the playwright's intent and to recognize the strategies used to achieve that intent.

A Structural Concept of Comedy, Tragedy, and Drama

Later we introduce a technique for analyzing a play's conflict, a system of structural analysis of a conflict and its resolution. During your first reading of a play, however, you should identify some essential structures that characterize most comedies and tragedies.

Comedies

Comedies tend to have one of two structures, each having to do with love, romance, and misunderstanding among the lovers: In romantic comedies (for example, most of Shakespeare's), two or more potential lovers become involved in a misunderstanding that must be rectified or clarified before they can be joined in marriage. In some other comedies (for example, most of Molière's), rather than focusing on the lovers and their misunderstandings, a greater focus is placed on a character who tries to keep the young lovers apart. Often there is a character, an older man, who lusts after a younger woman who is in love with a young man she wishes to marry. The older man serves as a comic "blocking" character. One way or another, in these blocking-character comedies, the young lovers are finally joined and the older man's selfishness is overcome, usually to his humiliation. Molière's *Tartuffe* is a comedy in which there is a blocking character. Tartuffe tries to marry Orgon's young daughter, who is betrothed to Valère.

Tragedies

The basic structure of tragedy has historically involved a central character who commits an act that has profoundly disruptive consequences. The central character's act produces disruption and suffering on her part and on the part of others. In turn, the central character's suffering leads her to perform some act that restores order; personal, community, political, even natural order are restored. Sophocles's *Antigone* and Shakespeare's *Hamlet* represent the characteristics we have ascribed here to tragedy.

Dramas

In modern times, especially since the last half of the nineteenth century, many plays have structures that are neither fully comic nor fully tragic. They are often called dramas. Wilson's *Joe Turner's Come and Gone* is such a play. There is romance, but it is not treated primarily in a comic manner; the play's emphasis is not on what or who keeps lovers apart. Likewise, the play's rhythm is not tragic; we do not see a character who struggles to the death trying to restore a political and social order.

A First Reading of *The Glass Menagerie*

Keep the questions below in mind as you read *The Glass Menagerie*, and return to them as soon as you finish reading, while the play is still fresh in your mind. Be sure to make notes of your impressions as you read and to highlight unfamiliar references. This will be your only first reading of *The Glass Menagerie*, so hold on to your impressions. They're valuable.

1. What is the play's story? From what sources did you learn the story? From dialogue? From stage directions?

   Tennessee Williams has created an unusual relationship that you must be especially aware of when reading this play the first time. Two voices in the written play frame the action. One is the voice of the playwright, Williams, provided through the stage directions. The other is the voice of Tom Wingfield, a character who also serves as the play's narrator. Attend to which information comes from the stage directions and which comes from Tom's narration. After reading the play, you should be able to identify how the two voices are similar and different (that is, Williams's voice speaking through the stage directions, and Tom's voice addressing us from the stage). You also should be able to identify where you learned what. That is, did you get information from stage directions, from Tom, or from dialogue?

2. Where and when is the play set? Where did you get the information? From stage directions? Dialogue?

3. What references may require research? Do not look up these references now. Simply note them and continue your first reading uninterrupted.

4. Who are the characters? How did you learn about them? From stage directions? From other characters' descriptions of them? From the characters' descriptions of themselves? From stage directions describing the characters' actions? From their dialogue? From their treatment of others? Attend to how you form impressions about characters. Class discussion of the play usually reveals surprisingly different reactions to each of *The Glass Menagerie*'s four characters.

5. Keep in mind that what characters say may or may not be true. Characters in plays are as undependable as people are in everyday life. If there's one thing we're all experts at, it's lying to others, especially about ourselves. We learned to do it at an early age, and we've had lots of practice.

6. What is the play's overall mood? Mostly serious? Comic? Tragic?

Questions for a First Reading of Any Play

1. What was your gut response to the play? Which characters seemed most interesting? Which least? What parts of the play really grabbed you? Which bored you?

2. What is the play's story? Review the basic plot.
3. What unfamiliar words or references did you encounter? Make a list for future research.
4. Make a diagram of the floor plan, if it is described.
5. Where and when is the play set? Where did you get the information? From stage directions? Dialogue?
6. Who are the characters and what is their relationship to each other? How did you learn about them? From stage directions? From other characters' descriptions of them? From the character's descriptions of themselves? From stage directions describing the characters' actions? From their dialogue? From their treatment of others?
7. What was the overall mood of the play? Mostly serious? Comic? Tragic?
8. Did you find yourself identifying with a particular character or characters? Lacking sympathy for others?

NOTE

[1] To avoid the awkwardness of using "his or her" throughout the text, we switch between the two terms in alternating chapters.

LEVEL TWO

The Essence of Drama

2

Conflict

The essence of drama is **conflict**, and without conflict there is no drama. This has long been a truism in the theatre. Poems, songs, short stories, and novels may create intense interest and achieve their essential purposes without conflict, but dramas (plays and films) cannot. For an event to be dramatic, conflict must exist between mutually opposing forces represented by characters whose goals and motives are sufficiently opposed that one of them cannot achieve his objectives without the others failing to achieve theirs. For a character to make a strong commitment to action he must have some important outcome he seeks, an immediate absence in his life that must be fulfilled. The more intensely he needs to achieve his objectives, the more ferociously he will struggle to achieve satisfaction. Drama grows out of opposing characters having profoundly important motives that they seek to fulfill. Out of the clash of these conflicting motives comes conflict, and the more immediately and profoundly the characters need to achieve their ideal futures, the more fuel goes into the fire of conflict.

The structure of the conflict affects how all other aspects of the play are understood. For instance, understanding the dramatic significance of the theatrical contract (Chapter 4) is enriched by recognizing whether protagonist or opposing force is addressing the audience and influencing the perception of the conflict. Therefore, if we are to understand profoundly the essential form of a play, we must understand its **conflict-resolution structure,** or the process through which the play attempts to resolve the conflict.

Not all conflicts end in a clear resolution, with one character succeeding and another failing in their attempts to achieve their goals. The ending may be ambiguous or may result in a stalemate. Nevertheless, this does not mean that the play lacks a conflict-resolution structure.

Concepts in Conflict Analysis

The following is a survey of the terms we use in conflict analysis. We first define these terms and then discuss how they can be used in conflict analysis.

Protagonist

In ancient Greek theatre two or three actors performed all of a play's speaking roles. The term *protagonist* applied both to the leading character and to the leading actor in a play.

In conflict analysis the **protagonist** is the character whose motives (needs a character seeks to fulfill) and actions (things a character does) drive the play's conflict from its beginning to its resolution. Beware: The title character is not always the protagonist. Although Hamlet is clearly the protagonist in William Shakespeare's play, it is doubtful that Tartuffe is the protagonist in Molière's *Tartuffe,* because he is not driving the play's conflict. Neither is the protagonist always the play's hero. No moral superiority is implied by being identified as the protagonist. Shakespeare's Richard III is the protagonist because his motives and actions drive the play's conflict, but he is in no way a hero.

Opposing Force

The play's conflict emerges when the protagonist's motives clash with the motives of an opposing force. Some play analysts use the term *antagonist* to refer to what we call **opposing force.** We have chosen not to use the term *antagonist* because of the connotations the word has acquired. The opposing force need not be a villain nor even someone who intentionally attempts to thwart the protagonist. However, the opposing force's motives and objectives are obstacles to the protagonist's goals and objectives. In Chapter 5 we will discuss the scene in *Romeo and Juliet* in which the title characters meet. In that scene Juliet is the opposing force for Romeo, because he is driving the action (trying to get a kiss), whereas she is an obstacle to that desire (by seeking to delay it). However, in the play as a whole, Juliet is not the opposing force. Individual scenes have their own conflict-resolution structure, a concept we discuss more fully in Chapter 6. At this point we are attempting to clarify the concepts of *protagonist* and *opposing force* as they apply to the total play's conflict-resolution process.

It is important to note that it is possible for the opposing force to be a group working together to prevent the protagonist from achieving his goal, rather than an individual. This is a rare occurrence, however, and it is best to proceed with your analysis under the assumption that there is a single opposing force.

A character, whether the protagonist or the opposing force, may want something desperately, so desperately the character is willing to do almost anything to achieve this objective. However, objectives usually are subject to conditions, or limitations, also known as **internal obstacles**. The protagonist may be willing to hurt others' feelings, perhaps permanently separating himself from someone he loves, but he may not be willing to murder to get what he wants. Internal obstacles are deeply involved in the character's sense of right and wrong, good and bad, pleasure and pain. Such obstacles are important to understanding the character's approach to achieving his goals. They complicate and deepen the external conflict. Therefore, when analyzing a character's motives, we might ask, within this conflict, what *internal* values or feelings stand in the way of the character achieving his goals?

The Structure of Dramatic Conflict

Introductory Incident

The **introductory incident** is the moment in the play when the *subject* of the conflict is introduced, in other words, the moment when the topic that the conflict is about is mentioned for the first time. An analogy: a boxing match. The point when the referee steps to the center of the ring and announces the upcoming bout is the introductory incident; it introduces the conflict that will form the basis of the match. In Sophocles's *Antigone*, the introductory incident comes in the opening scene between Antigone and Ismene, when Ismene asks if there is trouble and Antigone replies, "What else, when Creon singles out one brother / For a hero's grave, and lets the other rot?" This is the first mention of the subject of *Antigone*'s conflict: Creon's decision to bury one brother and disgrace the other. It is important to identify the introductory incident so that it can be given its appropriate emphasis in performance.

Moment of Engagement

The conflict's **moment of engagement** is the point when the protagonist commits to achieving his goals, the moment when he commits to satisfying his motives. From this moment on, the protagonist struggles to satisfy his motives despite the opposing forces. In the boxing match analogy, the bell rings signaling the bout's start, and the moment of engagement is when the boxers advance on each other. They are now committed to the fight, committed to their goal of winning. In *Hamlet*, the moment of engagement comes in Act I, Scene 5, when the Ghost asks Hamlet to kill Claudius, and he replies, "thy commandment all alone shall live / within the book and volume of my brain. . . ." From this moment on, Hamlet is committed to taking action, to killing Claudius. (Hamlet's *internal conflict* is that he needs to make sure that Claudius is actually guilty, and that he is not being tricked by a devil in the shape of his father's ghost.)

Climax

If there is a single most important moment in a play's conflict, it is the moment of **climax.** This is the moment when the conflict is resolved, when the protagonist achieves or fails to achieve his goals. At this moment, when it is clear he has won or lost, there is no longer conflict. The conflict has been resolved. When the knockout punch has been thrown and one of the downed boxers has been counted out, the climax has been achieved. There is a winner and a loser, and the match (the conflict) is over. If, however, the fight ends with no knockout punch thrown, and the winner is to be determined by the decision of the judges, the climax comes when the judges' decision is announced. In August Wilson's *Joe Turner's Come and Gone,* the climax comes when Loomis slashes himself across the chest with a knife, rubs the blood over his face, and "comes to a realization" that "I'm standing! I'm standing! My legs stood up! I'm standing now! Good-bye, Martha." And he exits. His search for his wife, and for his soul, has finally ended. The central conflict is resolved.

Denouement

The moments after the climax form the play's **denouement.** In these moments, misunderstandings are clarified, lovers are joined, or dead bodies are dragged offstage. The denouement in the boxing match includes those moments when the winner is congratulated by his trainers, the crowd cheers, and the loser is led away. The conflict has been resolved, no more punches will be thrown, and the main characters are enjoying or bemoaning the results of their actions. In *Tartuffe* we have to choose between two possible moments of climax. If the climax comes when the "Officer arrests Tartuffe" everything after the arrest (including the officer's long speech) is denouement. If the climax is judged to be the moment in which Orgon, persuaded by Cléante, finally stops pursuing Tartuffe, only the last four lines of the play serve as denouement.

Process for Determining the Conflict

The process of determining a play's conflict demands that we be systematic. Two of us may analyze a play and arrive at profoundly different conclusions. But the key is that our analyses be performed systematically. The process must employ both logic and intuition, and we must operate under the presumption that our answers are tentative, subject to repeated testing. Hans-Georg Gadamer's comment, taken from the study of literature, applies to our need to treat our analyses as exploratory: "the movement of understanding is constantly from the whole to the part and back to the whole.... The harmony of all the details with the whole is the criterion of correct understanding."[1] We ask, Does my analysis of the conflict's parts (protagonist, opposing force, introductory incident, moment of engagement, climax, and denouement) fit my sense of the play's whole? An analysis that fits logically but doesn't feel right intuitively must be questioned, reexamined. Although gut feelings should not be the sole basis for interpretation, neither should they be ignored. There is a sense of truth that rests in the emotions as well as in the intellect. Logic and the intuition should work together, ideally with a sense of their being elegantly appropriate to each other.

Moving Backward from the Climax

Conflict analysis begins after we have read the play and know how the plot's events transpired. Only when we know how the play has progressed from beginning to end can we pose the initial question of play analysis: At what moment does the conflict seem to be resolved? The moment when the conflict is resolved is the moment of climax. Ideally playwrights resolve their conflicts very near the play's end. When identifying a play's climax, we must be certain we are finding the conflict's last moment. One way to question, to challenge, our tentative decision about the climax is to ask whether important events transpire after the climax. Couples may announce their intent to marry after the moment of climax, or misunderstandings may be clarified, but a whole new cycle of conflict should not emerge after the climax. Generally speaking, if more than a few minutes are left after the proposed climax, we've probably made a mistake.

When we have tentatively identified the climax, we can pose a subsequent question: Who is the person who drove the conflict to this moment of climax? The character who drove the conflict to its resolution, its climax, is likely to be the play's protagonist.

Our answers to these two questions (At what moment does the conflict seem to be resolved? and Who is the person who drove the conflict to this moment of climax?) will determine our understanding of the play, so we must be certain our answers are supported by the whole of the text. If we ignore or discount factors that contradict our ideas, we will inevitably arrive at an interpretation that lacks coherence and dramatic effectiveness. In performance, the audience members may well sense something is wrong even if they cannot identify the source of their unease.

What Is the Major Dramatic Question?

One way to test a proposed climax is to ask, What question that has been pursued throughout the play is answered in the moment of climax? In the example of the boxing match, the question is a simple one: Who will win the fight? The **major dramatic question** in a play may be more complex, but it should be just as powerful and immediate. In addition, the major dramatic question should arise from the plot, not from thematic concerns.

There is nothing abstract about the major dramatic question. At its core it should restate the central preoccupation of all audience members: What is going to happen? For example, *Tartuffe*'s major dramatic question might be, Will Orgon give Tartuffe everything that he desires? For *Hamlet*, it might be, Will Hamlet justly revenge his father's death? Of course there are other, perhaps more elegant, ways to pose these plays' major dramatic questions, but what is important is that we ask the question directly and powerfully. We should be comfortable with the climax we've identified. Then we ask, What major dramatic question was answered in the moment of climax? Climax and question ought to feel like they're a perfect fit.

The major dramatic question always takes the same format: Will [the protagonist] _____? Will Hamlet justly revenge his father's death? Will Dorothy (in *The Wizard of Oz*) get back home? In other words, it always is phrased in terms of the play's protagonist, and in terms of the plot.

The best way to double-check the validity of your major dramatic question is to rephrase it as the protagonist's primary objective for the play. In other words, convert "Will [the protagonist] _____?" into "[The protagonist] wants to _____." For example, if the major dramatic question of *Hamlet* is "Will Hamlet justly revenge his father's death?," then it converts to "Hamlet wants to justly revenge his father's death." Then ask yourself, Could this reasonably serve as Hamlet's primary objective for the play? If yes, then you have a useful major dramatic question; if not, you need to rethink it.

This process helps overcome the tendency to create major dramatic questions that are thematic or judgmental. One of the authors received from a student an analysis of *Death of a Salesman* that stated the major dramatic question as "Will Willy finally realize the falseness of his values and philosophy?" While this question is an important theme in the play, converting it into the protagonist's main objective reveals its problem: "Willy wants to realize the falseness of his values and philosophy." Back to the drawing board.

Further Testing of the Analysis

When we have tentatively identified (a) the climax, (b) the protagonist, and (c) the major dramatic question, we are ready to return to the play's beginning. Now we ask three additional questions:

1. At what moment is the subject of the conflict introduced? This is the introductory incident. Just as it is ideal for the climax to come near the play's end, with a few moments remaining after the conflict is resolved, it is ideal for the introductory moment to come early in the play, thus filling the play with conflict from beginning to end.
2. At what moment does the protagonist commit irrevocably to achieving his motives, to fulfilling his goals, to overcoming the

forces that oppose him? This is the moment of engagement. As with the introductory incident, it is ideal for the moment of commitment to come early in the play, thus filling the play with commitment to resolution. By having Hamlet commit to revenge early in the play, in his first meeting with the Ghost, Shakespeare has created an early moment of engagement, filling the play with conflict from beginning to end.

3. Who is the character who opposes the protagonist? That character is the opposing force.

Identifying the play's introductory moment, choosing the protagonist's moment of engagement, and clarifying the opposing forces are critical to understanding the conflict's trajectory and to organizing a production in a fashion that fully emphasizes the play's conflict. In performance we probably won't choose to underline these moments or elements in such a way that they are obvious to an audience, but if we are to communicate fully the play's essence, we must be clear about the play's central element—its conflict—and its key structural moments. Because the conflict is the play's animating element, these key structural elements must receive their appropriate emphasis in performance.

Conflict in *The Glass Menagerie*

Up to now we have tried to guide your thinking about *The Glass Menagerie* by posing questions while allowing you to arrive at your own answers. But at this point in our study of conflict analysis, we're going to propose a possible analysis and leave it to you, your classmates, and your instructor to propose alternative analyses. We do this because we have learned in the classroom that in applying conflict analysis for the first time, it is important for you to have a proposed analysis to which you can react, and we believe the process of verification and justification is as important as the answers themselves. Therefore, to demonstrate the process, we propose tentative answers.

Questions about the Climax

To locate the climax, we ask, At what moment in *The Glass Menagerie* is the conflict resolved? We consider Tom's speeches that open and close the play to be framing devices that provide a context for the play's conflict. So the climax must come in a moment before Tom's final speech. We suggest that the climax lies in the final confrontation between Amanda and Tom in Scene 7. Tom threatens to leave, saying, "I'll go, and I won't go to the movies," to which Amanda responds, "Go, then! Go to the moon—you selfish dreamer!"

1. Can this moment be the play's climax?

   It may be. There is no further dialogue among the family members, so there doesn't seem to be an opportunity for further conflict among the characters. If this is the climax, who is the person who drove the conflict to this climax?

2. If Amanda is the protagonist, what has she sought?

   Has she achieved or failed to achieve her goals? If Tom is the protagonist, what has he sought, and has he gotten what he wanted?

Questions about the Major Dramatic Question

1. What major dramatic question is answered when Amanda tells Tom to "go to the moon" and Tom leaves? Let's review some of Amanda's struggles with Tom in preceding scenes, scenes in which she addresses her motives and objectives.

   Has Amanda struggled to keep Tom from leaving home? Yes. Was she asking him to stay in order to take care of her in her old age? Perhaps, but she never says so. In fact, she declares earlier in the play that she's not concerned about herself. Has Amanda been asking Tom to stay on at the shoe factory until she can marry Laura to someone who would look after her? If we are to trust Amanda's words, the answer is yes: She has sought a gentleman caller for Laura in order to take care of her daughter's future. So, a possible major dramatic question is, Will Amanda get Tom to stay home, working in the shoe factory, until she and Tom find Laura a gentleman caller to marry, a man to care for Laura and provide Amanda with the comfort of knowing Laura is all right? Or, to state it more succinctly, Will Amanda keep Tom at home, involved in seeking the security of a husband for Laura? If transformed into Amanda's main objective, it reads: Amanda wants to keep Tom at home, involved in seeking the security of a husband for Laura. That seems to be Amanda's primary desire.

Questions for Testing Our Proposed Climax and Major Dramatic Question

Let's propose (again, still tentatively) that the climax is Amanda's line, "Go, then! Go to the moon—you selfish dreamer!" And let's assume the major dramatic question is, Can Amanda keep Tom at home, involved in seeking the security of a husband for Laura? We can test our theory by answering a few other questions:

1. What is the introductory incident?

   This is the moment in which the subject of the conflict is introduced, so we must ask, When does Amanda introduce her desire to seek a gentleman caller and husband for Laura? Perhaps in Scene 1 when Amanda says, "I want you to stay fresh and pretty—for gentleman callers!" Yes, Laura dismisses the possibility, but the subject of a husband for Laura has been broached, and Amanda expands on it by describing her seventeen gentleman callers.

2. What is the moment of engagement?

This is the moment when the protagonist commits to overcoming the forces that oppose her. So, when does Amanda commit to the pursuit of a gentleman caller for Laura?

It may be in Scene 2: After confronting Laura about her deception, after describing the lives of poor Southern spinsters, and after talking about Jim O'Connor, Amanda announces, "Girls that aren't cut out for business careers usually wind up married to some nice man. *[Gets up with a spark of revival.]* Sister, that's what you'll do!"

The play supports this as Amanda's moment of irrevocable commitment. At the beginning of the next scene, Tom describes Amanda's determination to lure a gentleman caller: "It became an obsession. Like some archetype of the universal unconscious, the image of the gentleman caller haunted our small apartment." The rest of the play, in fact, deals with preparations for the arrival of the gentleman caller and for what happens when he visits.

Notice how we are gathering evidence from a variety of places in the play, so that our answers have support from the whole of the play. It can be self-deceptive to base your analysis on a small part of the play and ignore evidence from other parts. Be sure that no evidence elsewhere seems to contradict what you are proposing.

3. Do the proposed introductory incident, moment of engagement, and climax support the major dramatic question we have proposed?

If these elements relate coherently and if they fit with each other—and in our opinion, they do—we may have arrived at a conflict analysis of *The Glass Menagerie*.

However, some analysts have proposed Tom as the play's protagonist, and others have asserted that the play is about Laura. Can a coherent conflict analysis be built around Tom as the play's protagonist? How about Laura as the protagonist? Does either Tom or Laura drive the conflict, making the dramatic action intense?

4. How shall we account for Tom's opening and closing speeches?

When we began looking for the play's climax, we set aside Tom's opening and closing speeches, asserting they were framing devices that provide a context for the conflict. However, they can't be ignored permanently. How can our analysis, proposing that Amanda is the protagonist, account for Tom's opening and closing speeches? We view Tom's opening speech as something that provides a political and social setting for the play, preparing us for the play's poetic and nonrealistic nature but lacking an obvious set of goals that will be opposed directly in the play.

The closing speech relates Tom to the conflict: He has left home. He articulates his guilt over abandoning Laura and tells us how he can't get her out of his mind. If his speech, "Blow out your candles, Laura—and so goodbye ... ," were the play's climax, we would have to double back and ask, When did he introduce the subject of his abandoning her (introductory incident)? When did he commit to resolving that question (moment of engagement)? What is the major dramatic question that this conflict pursued and answered in this proposed moment of climax?

Some analysts may argue that Tom is the protagonist because he introduces the subject of the play, brings home the gentleman caller, and finally abandons his mother and his sister. They might say that makes him the protagonist. That proposition would require an alternative analysis, one that identifies a different set of conflict moments: introductory incident, moment of commitment, climax, and major dramatic question. A key question regarding Tom as protagonist is, Has his struggle to stay (or leave) been the play's central conflict?

Questions about the Conflict-Resolution Structure in Any Play

1. Who is the protagonist?
2. Which characters are the protagonist's opposing forces?
3. What is the climax?
4. What is the major dramatic question?
5. What is the introductory incident?
6. What is the moment of engagement?
7. Do the proposed introductory incident, moment of engagement, and climax support the major dramatic question?

NOTE

[1] Quoted in Ken Wilber, *The Eye of Spirit* (Boston: Shambhala Publications, Inc., 2001), p. 87.

LEVEL THREE

Gathering Information

3

Given Circumstances

Play analysts attempt to understand the world in which the characters live: the information they share, the time and place in which they live, the social systems that affect them, and other cultural factors that influence their world. These are the play's **given circumstances,** a term coined by Constantin Stanislavsky.

Given circumstances refers to information (stage directions and dialogue) that provides the characters' environment. We use four categories to organize this information:

- Events and relationships that precede the play or, to borrow from the language of film and television, the backstory
- The play's when and where: its period in history, its specific time and place
- The social systems that affect the characters: the political, economic, and religious systems that underlie the society within which the play is set
- Cultural norms that shape the characters' attitudes toward race, class, gender, family, love and marriage, and language use

These four divisions are, of course, somewhat arbitrary and in practice tend to overlap. For example, families exist within political, economic, and religious systems. But the categories help ensure that all elements of given circumstances are identified and clarified.

Given Circumstances: Stated and Implied

Given circumstances may be stated explicitly, requiring only that we attend to them, or they may be implied, requiring us to deduce what may be important information. In Chapter 1 we quoted extensively from a lengthy example of stated given circumstances: August Wilson's stage directions at the beginning of *Joe Turner's Come and Gone*. Wilson goes to some extreme in stating or identifying the given circumstances. He describes the play's social setting, its time, the location, the characters' backgrounds, even the setting's doors and where they lead. In other instances, given circumstances may be implied: In the opening scene of Molière's *Tartuffe* (a play that builds its conflict partly on the subject of religious hypocrisy), religion is mentioned, but it is merely assumed that the religion is Christianity. A Roman Catholic king, Louis XIV, ruled France at the time of the play's premiere, but Christianity isn't mentioned until the second act, and Roman Catholicism (or its offshoot, Jansenism, which may have been Molière's target) is never mentioned explicitly in the play. In fact, the text doesn't even mention that the play is set in Paris; it is implied.

Analysis demands a thorough, detailed understanding of the given circumstances. Rather than depending on memory, we believe in keeping careful notes regarding these specifics. At the end of the chapter we provide a format for taking notes, one that we believe you will find useful.

Accuracy and Given Circumstances

To some degree, analysis of given circumstances demands that we interpret the playwright's intent: Does the playwright create a world in which the historical, geographic, social, and cultural circumstances are to be treated literally? Or does the playwright seem to seek an understanding that these factors are treated loosely?

William Shakespeare wrote at a time before playwrights were expected to observe literal historical or geographical accuracy. Sometimes he combined two or more historical individuals into a single dramatic character. Sometimes he collapsed historical events that had transpired over several years into what, within the context of the plot, seems a period of a few days. Anachronism (misplacing historical events) is common in Shakespeare; for example, a line in his *Julius Caesar* refers to a clock striking when, in fact, clocks had not been invented in Caesar's time. Even though there was no seacoast of Bohemia, it doesn't preclude Shakespeare from giving Bohemia a seacoast in *The Winter's Tale*.

Modern and contemporary plays, especially those written in the nineteenth century and after, tend to be much more historically accurate than are plays of earlier times. Whether playwrights state or imply given circumstances, we must determine how literally they intend for the information to be read.

Research Sources

Play analysts soon realize the need for inventive research. As play analysts we have found ourselves reading novels set in a play's time; searching in magazines for photographs of modern events such as the Irish Rebellion; reading Wikipedia on French history, culture, and art for productions of Molière; and viewing a film of Henry Fielding's *Tom Jones* and looking at Hogarth drawings, employing both the film and the drawings as sources for a production of a Shakespearean play set in eighteenth-century England. Imagination, resourcefulness, and the aid of reference librarians are absolute requirements for play analysts.

Backstory: Events and Relationships that Precede the Play

In almost every play, events and relationships have happened before the play begins. Perhaps wars have been fought, loves or hatreds have begun or ended, family members have been born or died, or institutions and organizations have risen or fallen. These preceding events, which are part of the given circumstances, may be called exposition, or the **backstory**. These events and relationships *must be alluded to within the play* or they are not given circumstances. For example, Hamlet grew up at court as the son of King Hamlet. As a boy he probably had someone who tutored him in reading, writing, and arithmetic, but because tutoring isn't mentioned in the play, it's not part of the given circumstances. In contrast, Hamlet's father died before the play begins. Because characters in the play talk about King Hamlet's death and the events surrounding it, his death and its related events are very much part of the given circumstances.

Play analysts assume that if the playwright intended the information as part of the given circumstances, he would have implied it or included it in either the dialogue or the stage directions. Actors who create or invent events or relationships not mentioned in the play may find such inventions enriching to their performance, but they must be aware that they are creating a fiction they are contributing to the play, and that these events shouldn't be confused with the given circumstances the playwright provided. In other words, these creations or inventions shouldn't influence the play's interpretation.

Setting: The Play's When and Where

Play analysis demands that we understand the time and place of the action.

Studying the play's historical period may provide the backstory for the characters. For example, Shakespeare's *Richard III* is set during the title character's brief reign: 1483–1485. As play analysts, we would use this information to research the challenges Richard faced and to identify the probable scope of his powers. We would learn from historical research that when Richard III assumed the throne England had undergone almost a century of wars over the kingship (the War of the Roses). We would learn that in secular matters, Englishmen served the king, whereas in religious matters they respected the power and wisdom of the Roman Catholic Church and its pope.

In addition to researching a period play's historical time frame, we must look for both stated and implied information about the specific time when the play takes place: the season of the year and the time of day. If it is set in summer in a temperate zone above the equator, we can assume the playwright wanted us to think of hot weather. If it takes place at midnight, we can assume it's dark outdoors. This information might be important to lighting designers, for instance, when deciding on the color, intensity, and direction of light; or, it might be useful to costume designers when designing clothing to suit the season and time of day.

The place in which the play's events occur may also be critical to understanding the action. It would be almost impossible to understand Irish playwright John Millington Synge's one-act tragedy *Riders to the Sea*, for example, without being aware of the dangerous geography of the Aran Islands, in which the play is set.

Specifics of location may be meaningful for either invoking or debunking stereotypes. In plays written during the English Restoration, for example, the difference between the city and the country was emphasized, with city dwellers assumed to be more sophisticated. It is important to know what is implied, for example, by the setting of George Farquhar's *The Beaux' Stratagem*, which takes place in an inn in Lichfield, an English backwater town, as opposed to fashionable London. In other plays, the country is stereotyped as purer than the city (even Kansas City, as in Rodgers and Hammerstein's *Oklahoma!*). We must examine every play for its stated and implied information about the play's locale and the information, including stereotypes, the playwright meant to invoke through choice of place.

Social Systems that Affect the Characters

The terms *social* and *society* refer to the ways people live in relationship to each other. Clearly politics, economics, and religion interact to create much of what is thought of as a society or a social system. A social *system* tends to be made up of institutions and structures (for instance, the legal system is made up of the courts, the laws, the police officers, the lawyers, and so forth). Such matters as politics and religion may be important in one play and relatively unimportant in another. A play may be set on an island where politics is thought of as something far removed from the characters' consciousness. Or a play may be organized around a religious war, making matters of religion and politics central to analyzing its given circumstances. Characters' relative wealth or poverty may be a play's central issue, or economics may be an unimportant topic that never comes up. Also, characters' economic status may be implied or assumed rather than stated overtly.

A play's social and religious setting can be critically important. In ancient Greek tragedies the chorus is often made up of "citizens" whose speeches represent the community's political, social, and religious points of view. Often the leading character, the protagonist, of Greek tragedies is a person who has violated one or more of the community's standards of conduct, and the chorus comments on the resultant punishment the protagonist or the community is likely to suffer. The chorus also comments on the gods' expectations of humans. This is the case in Sophocles's *Antigone*.

Cultural Norms

In other plays politics, economics, and religion are less important than social standards. These standards, or cultural norms, exist more at the level of the individual rather than the institutions that make up social systems. For example, in some plays the cultural norm is for men to have mistresses, but it is understood that such conduct is maintained with the utmost of privacy and discretion. When the social rule of discretion is violated, families and communities are offended. Again, these concerns may be stated in dialogue or stage directions, or they may be implied and require that we research the social norms common to the play's setting.

Attitudes Regarding Ethnicity

Play analysis demands that we consider carefully the implications of ethnicity. For example, in American plays of the nineteenth century we can assume that middle-class and upper-class characters are prejudiced toward the Irish, stereotyping them as ruddy faced, hard drinking, Catholic, uncouth, and uneducated. But late-twentieth-century plays for the most part avoid those prejudicial stereotypes while exhibiting others.

Early twentieth-century American plays assume strong prejudice against ethnic and religious intermarriage; however, by the beginning of the twenty-first century, intermarriage has become much more commonplace. Each play demands its own search for attitudes, some stated and some unstated.

Attitudes Regarding Marriage, Family, and the Sexes

When analyzing a play, we can't assume that the play's characters share our personal attitudes about marriage and family, or love and sex.

Attitudes toward marriage and family have varied immensely over time, with romantic love becoming increasingly important in Western culture. Centuries ago there was a common assumption that parents arranged their children's marriages, with social and economic factors being more important to the parents than the question of whether the bride and groom were in love. Family wealth was passed down, generation to generation, through marriage and dowries; money and position were often more important than romantic love. This is the case in *Tartuffe*, for example. Today there are cultures and families in which these traditions are maintained.

Similarly, cultures have varied throughout history in their attitudes toward premarital and extramarital sex. Some assume that brides must be virgins; others assume that brides will have experimented sexually. In Shakespeare's time it seems to have been accepted for a couple to engage in sexual activity before the wedding but only after they had formally announced their intention to wed. Other cultures have considered polygamy to be the social norm.

Even something like clothing can reflect cultural norms. In the America of the 1930s, for instance, it was a sign of rebellion for a woman to wear slacks instead of a dress. In a play such as Philip Barry's *The Philadelphia Story*, for instance, the central character, Tracy Lord, is not only divorced but also wears slacks, a sign that she is in revolt against the dominant cultural norms regarding a woman's "place."

Attitudes about marriage, family, and the sexes will be stated or implied in stage directions or dialogue. Read carefully, and do not apply your own values and attitudes to the text.

Language Use

Play analysts learn about characters and their given circumstances through the characters' language; therefore, it is critically important for us to be skillful observers and interpreters of characters' speech.

Playwrights often imply characters' education and social class through language. Shakespeare frequently introduces characters who misuse language in a comical fashion; they are uneducated, lower-class folks who try to imitate the educated, upper class. The term *malapropism* was coined to describe the misuse of words to humorous effect: Mrs. Malaprop is a character in Richard Brinsley Sheridan's 1775 play, *The Rivals*. An example of a malapropism is "an allegory on the banks of the Nile."

In British plays, characters are often stereotyped by dialect and pronunciation, perhaps more so than they are in American plays. British playwrights give characters social class accents that are immediately recognizable stereotypes that British audiences pick up on. Regional accents are less commonly used by American playwrights as indicators of either social class or education, although the use of Southern dialect is a common outlier.

American playwrights more often provide character information through the use of proper and improper grammar, with the implication that those who use language incorrectly are less educated, perhaps persons of lower class status.

Plays in Translation

Play analysts will encounter texts that have been translated into English from other languages. In fact, a list of "great" plays in Western theatrical history probably will include a majority of plays originating in other languages. We can be certain that translation has, to some degree, changed meaning.

Sometimes, a translator will attempt to find parallels to reflect cultural stereotypes in the original. For instance, Douglass Parker's translation of *Lysistrata* by the ancient Greek comic playwright Aristophanes used an American Southern dialect for the lines spoken by the Spartan characters, drawing a parallel between the Athenian attitude toward their uncouth neighbors and the American attitude toward Southern country folk.

Notable differences exist between plays translated by British and American writers. Until the second half of the twentieth century, translations of major playwrights such as Ibsen, Strindberg, Molière, and Chekov were available mostly in versions by British translators; in recent years more of these playwrights' works have been translated by Americans. We advise comparing multiple translations.

Plays in Fantastical Settings

Many plays are not set in real places or real times; they are set in fantasy places and times. Nevertheless, they still have given circumstances, albeit invented ones. Obviously traditional research is impossible in such cases (no historical or geographical reference points exist); therefore, the given circumstances must be gleaned from a close analysis of the text. The process of searching for the given circumstances, interpreting them, and identifying the questions that must be asked of the text will be similar to that of a play set in a historical period or geographical place that is totally unfamiliar. However, unlike researching a historical play, all information must be derived from the play. No outside sources exist to which the analyst can refer. Fantastical plays require skillful study of their given circumstances.

Plays Emphasize Different Given Circumstances

Consider three plays we will be drawing from for our examples throughout the book: Sophocles's *Antigone,* Molière's *Tartuffe,* and August Wilson's *Joe Turner's Come and Gone.* Each play is profoundly different from the others in the categories of given circumstances that are critical to its **plot** and its conflict.

In *Antigone* the backstory is central to both the plot and the conflict. In a battle that precedes the play, Antigone's brothers, Eteocles and Polynices, killed each other. And, before the play, Creon decreed that Eteocles be buried with honors; whereas he decreed that Polynices be treated as a traitor who must lie unburied, his soul desecrated. The conflict grows out of these important events that precede the play.

Tartuffe's backstory is relatively insignificant in comparison with *Antigone*'s. Admittedly, Orgon and his mother have fallen under Tartuffe's influence before the play begins, but the plot and conflict center on Orgon's blindness to Tartuffe's religious hypocrisy, which is demonstrated in action before the audience. Past events are less important than the events the audience sees.

For most of *Joe Turner*'s characters, preceding events are less important than social and economic factors that affect the play's action. Admittedly, before the play Loomis was kidnapped and forced to work on a chain gang for seven years, after which he returned to find his wife gone. He has been searching for her ever since. But most of *Joe Turner*'s characters engage in onstage struggles that the audience observes, struggles growing out of segregation and poverty. Events preceding the play affect the characters only to a limited extent.

Gathering Information on Given Circumstances in *The Glass Menagerie*

The Glass Menagerie is a modern American play, written and produced originally in the 1940s. Paradoxically it is a play that addresses issues familiar to us today, yet it is set in a time that is unfamiliar to many. It requires research into US history and culture and asks us to consider the similarities and differences between today's America and the America of the 1930s and 1940s. It demands that we, as play analysts, project ourselves into times, places, and experiences that many of us have heard of, but about which we may know little.

To demonstrate the process of analyzing a period play's given circumstances, we explain here some of the play's given circumstances in detail and we identify references that require research. Our focus is on

Chapter 3 ■ Given Circumstances   45

information conveyed in the early parts of the play, but obviously this process must extend throughout the play, demanding that we unearth all the information that constitutes the play's given circumstances.

Questions about the Backstory

1. What important events precede the play? Where do you learn about these preceding events? What do you learn from stage directions? What do you learn from dialogue?
2. What information do you get about Tom's father? How long ago did he leave? How old were Tom and Laura then? What were the circumstances of his departure?

    You enjoy a privileged position in relationship to the characters: You have information they don't; you know things they don't know, including how the play ends. You must keep track of how you gathered this information and why they don't have it.

3. What does Laura know about Tom that Amanda doesn't know? What does Tom know about Jim that neither Amanda nor Laura knows? This question becomes especially important when Tom must confess to not knowing Jim was engaged to be married.

Questions about Setting

Time

Tennessee Williams's initial stage directions tell us when the play takes place: *"Time—Now and the Past."* *The Glass Menagerie* was produced originally in Chicago in December 1944 and in New York City in March 1945. The play's "Now," we can infer, is 1944–1945, at the end World War II.

Tom's opening monologue gives specifics about when the play's events take place. Tom is speaking in the present time of the mid-1940s and will tell about events from his past:

> Tom: To begin with, I turn back time. I reverse it to that quaint period, the thirties, when the huge middle class of America was matriculating in a school for the blind. Their eyes had failed them, or they had failed their eyes, and so they were having their fingers pressed forcibly down on the fiery Braille alphabet of a dissolving economy.
>
> In Spain there was revolution. Here there was only shouting and confusion. In Spain there was Guernica. Here there were disturbances of labor, sometimes pretty violent, in otherwise peaceful cities such as Chicago, Cleveland, Saint Louis. . . . This is the social background of the play.

1. What parts of the play take place in "Now"? What parts take place in "the Past"? What were the major events in St. Louis during those periods? In the United States? In the world?
2. To what do the terms "Guernica" and the "Spanish Revolution" refer? How did American intellectuals and artists feel about Guernica and the Spanish Revolution?
3. What kinds of "disturbances of labor" were taking place? Were there also race riots? Why might Williams refer to one and not the other?
4. How did Americans in 1944–1945, the time of the play's performance (the play's "Now"), feel differently about their own time than they felt about the 1930s?
5. Can you identify each scene's time of year? Time of day?
6. How much time passes between scenes? How much time has passed between the events shown within the play and the speeches that Tom makes to begin the play?

Place

Williams provides a location for the play's opening: *"SCENE—An alley in St. Louis."* His extensive, initial stage directions tell us more about the location:

> The Wingfield apartment is in the rear of the building, one of those vast hive-like conglomerations of cellular living-units that flower as warty growths in over-crowded urban centers of lower-middle-class population and are symptomatic of the impulse of this largest and fundamentally enslaved section of American society to avoid fluidity and differentiation and to exist and function as one interfused mass of automatism.
>
> The apartment faces an alley and is entered by a fire-escape, a structure whose name is a touch of accidental poetic truth, for all of these huge buildings are always burning with the slow and implacable fires of human desperation. The fire-escape is included in the set—that is, the landing of it and steps descending from it.

1. St. Louis is located on the eastern side of Missouri, a Midwestern state that borders on the Mississippi River. Is the absence of an ocean important in any way? Is it more important to one character than to others?
2. The play is set outside and inside a tenement apartment. How and why is this important? It will be worthwhile to research the term *tenement*, both for its literal meaning and for its economic and social implications. Is it possible to find out what an inner-city tenement in St. Louis in the 1930s was like? Are there photographs of such places?

3. Tom and Jim work in a shoe factory. How was industry important to the St. Louis economy of the 1930s? What industries were important?

Questions about Social Systems that Affect the Characters

Political Systems

Williams's stage directions refer to the political and economic environment of the 1930s. There are references to the "middle-class population," as the "largest and fundamentally enslaved section of American society" avoiding "fluidity and differentiation" existing and functioning "as one interfused mass of automatism." Were American attitudes toward the working class different in the 1930s and 1940s than they are today? In the context of the Great Depression, many Americans were fighting for the right to organize into labor unions, challenging the legitimacy of the country's historical roots in capitalism, advocating socialism and even communism as alternatives to the nation's economic and social organization. Today collective social organization is no longer a mainstream impulse. It is important to analyze the play with these differences in mind. How have attitudes toward collective action changed since the 1930s? Why?

In Scene V, Part One, Tom's monologue opens with references to the Paradise Dance Hall, its music, its couples, and impending change. But then he turns to the global political situation:

> Tom: Adventure and change were imminent in this year. They were waiting around the corner for all those kids. Suspended in the mist over Berchtesgaden, caught in the folds of Chamberlain's umbrella—In Spain there was Guernica! But here there was only hot swing music and liquor, dance halls, bars, and movies, and sex that hung in the gloom like a chandelier and flooded the world with brief, deceptive rainbows.... All the world was waiting for bombardments!

1. Tom suggests the young people at the Paradise Dance Hall were paying little attention to political events in Europe. Was this typical of Americans at the time? What were the American attitudes toward Europe and war?
2. What was Berchtesgaden? What was Berchtesgaden's relationship to "Chamberlain's umbrella"?

These references, like the references to Guernica, are allusions to social and political events that preceded America's entry into World War II. To analyze the play profoundly, we must understand Tom's speech about the Paradise Dance Hall. We must understand the interplay among the dance hall, the music, the sex, the young people's lack of adventure, the feelings and behavior of the lower middle classes, and the politics of the impending war. This requires research and contemplation.

Economic Systems

The play refers to the effects of the Great Depression on employment in the 1930s and 1940s. Today's systems for protecting the poor (Medicaid, food stamps, and departments of children and family services) were, for the most part, not yet in place. In the 1930s, private charities attended to many needs that are met today by state and federal government programs.

1. Many Americans found themselves unemployed for long periods during the Great Depression. How does the nationwide unemployment problem affect the play's characters? How do the economic times affect Tom, Laura, and Amanda differently?
2. Amanda has no job. How were employment conditions different in the 1930s for women than for men? How does this affect the Wingfields?
3. Are Jim's attitudes toward money and economics different from those of the Wingfields? Jim seems to be devoted to self-improvement; he is taking a night school course in public speaking. Does this reflect a desire on his part to improve himself economically? What does his interest in the future of television reflect? His interest in communication? In science? One of the most popular American books of the 1930s was Dale Carnegie's *How to Win Friends and Influence People*. Could Jim's interests reflect Carnegie's ideas?

Religious Systems

The play has many religious references. But some may require amplification, for example, Jim's being Roman Catholic. America in the 1930s had a culture and social system dominated by Protestant Christianity. In 1928 there was a Roman Catholic candidate for president of the United States, the former governor of New York state, Al Smith. His Catholicism played a role in his defeat.

1. Are there religious references that help you understand the characters' beliefs, attitudes, and given circumstances? Consider, for example, references to the birth of Jesus, clergy, candelabra, the Annunciation, the risen Christ, the Virgin Mary, altar candles, Christian adults, El Diablo, prayer, Paradise, and Moses.
2. For which characters is Christianity a major motivating force in their lives?
3. How might you distinguish between religious references in the stage directions and religious references in the dialogue?

Questions about Cultural Norms

Attitudes Regarding Ethnicity

During the period after World War II, the United States saw monumental changes in attitudes and laws regarding racial or ethnic discrimi-

Chapter 3 ■ Given Circumstances   49

nation. As late as the 1960s many examples of discrimination were tolerated: in some regions, separate drinking fountains for Whites and Blacks, exclusion of ethnic minorities (Blacks and Jews especially) from residential areas, and racially segregated schools. In the 1960s, national legislation was passed making many discriminatory practices illegal. Since the 1970s, employment practices have changed, making it illegal to discriminate against hiring someone on the basis of race, religion, or gender.

1. How is race or ethnicity important to the play's given circumstances?
2. Amanda talks of herself as having grown up in the South. She makes racially insensitive remarks about people of color. Were her attitudes toward race and ethnicity common in the St. Louis of the play's setting? How do Tom and Laura seem to relate to race and racial difference?
3. Does Williams want us to see Amanda as racist? Does he intend that we see her as a person from a different culture from her children's?
4. Jim is Irish and Catholic. Does this make a difference to Amanda? To Tom? To Laura?

Attitudes Regarding Marriage, Family, and the Sexes

In some ways, today's American practices and attitudes toward marriage and family differ from those of the 1930s and 1940s. For example, the percentage of marriages that end in divorce has increased. Legal protections for abandoned spouses and children are different. Today many women expect to work outside the home, and middle-class wives are more likely than Amanda to have prepared themselves to earn a living. Analysis of *The Glass Menagerie* requires researching issues of marriage and family in the 1930s.

1. Amanda is a member of the D.A.R. (Daughters of the American Revolution). What does this tell us about her family background? Also, what were the D.A.R.'s attitudes toward ethnicity and economics?
2. Amanda and Jim seem to have attitudes toward marriage and family that differ from Tom's and Laura's. What are the differences, and how might we account for them?
3. Much of *The Glass Menagerie*'s plot and its conflict revolve around Tom's impulse to leave the family home and Amanda's demand that he stay until Laura's future is ensured. Might this conflict be different if the play were set in today's America? How do the circumstances of the 1930s affect this issue of Tom's staying or leaving?

Language Use

Language reflects identity, motives, thought process, relationships, and culture; in other words, language reflects every aspect of human beings in their given circumstances. American language has changed along with other aspects of culture and society; some people believe that in the age of film, television, and the Internet American culture has diminished, perhaps these media have debased, the importance of language. If that is so, it is especially important that play analysts develop heightened sensitivities to language.

1. How do the characters use language in ways that are similar to or different from the people you know? Do they have different vocabularies? Do they use wider or more limited vocabularies?
2. Do they speak in longer or shorter sentences than you, your friends, and your family? Do they use more specific or less specific language than the people you know?
3. Do they use language that is more formal or less formal than the people with whom you associate? Is the play's informal language different from the informal language you use and hear today?
4. How does Williams use language to differentiate among the four characters? In other words, how do you learn about these people by studying their language?
5. Does one character use profanity more than others? Does one use religious imagery more than others? Is one more poetic than the others? Does one speak in a manner that reflects passivity? Activity? Does one use the language of business and commerce more than others? These are but a few of the kinds of questions about language that are demanded in the analysis of given circumstances.

Questions about Given Circumstances in Any Play

1. What are the events and relationships that precede the play? How do you learn about them?
2. What are the play's when and where: its period in history, its specific time and place?
3. What social systems most affect the characters?
4. What are the play's most important attitudes regarding race, class, and gender?
5. What are the cultural conditions and assumptions that shape the characters' attitudes regarding family, love and marriage, education, and language?
6. Which given circumstances seem to have the greatest effect on the play as a whole?
7. Which given circumstances seem to have the greatest effect on the major characters?

Organizing Information about Given Circumstances

Using the following categories, you could record on 3"-by-5" index cards the information you find. If you prefer, you can do this in a computer database, which will allow for even more detailed and faster searches.

- *Page* number where the reference is found
- *Subject* of the reference
- *Category* of the reference (for example, events and relationships that precede the play; the when and where of the play, the systems that affect the characters, cultural norms.)
- *Source* (Was the information found in stage directions, or was it spoken by a character?)
- *Details* (Elaborate on the background of the reference.)

Once you have categorized your given circumstances, you can sort them in a variety of ways. Perhaps you are looking for all the references to ethnicity in the play or are searching for all the when and where details of the play. Sort out all the cards that pertain to these subjects and review them as a group.

4

Theatrical Contract

In this chapter we analyze how a production forms a **theatrical contract** with its audience. A theatrical contract is an informal understanding or agreement between a theatrical production and its audience. Unlike formal contracts agreed upon between two or more parties before work begins, the theatrical contract evolves as the play proceeds.

Establishing a theatrical contract may be compared to establishing a poker hand's rules: Before distributing the cards the dealer must announce the version of the game to be played (perhaps Five Card Draw) and the wild cards (perhaps aces wild). We might say that the dealer has established a "poker contract," that is, the rules to be followed in the game.

Similarly, in the theatre the director, actors, and designers establish the production's rules based on their reading of the script. Unlike in the card game, however, the theatrical contract's rules are not announced explicitly or overtly; rather the audience gathers them unconsciously, surmising them from the information it receives during the performance, usually in its first moments.

Each production of a play creates its own unique contract that is shaped by the artistic choices made by each member of the production team. Audiences seem willing to accept most contracts offered them as long as the rules are clear and consistent. Inconsistency breeds confusion and hinders the audience from fully experiencing the intended world of the play. Ideally the production team will have communicated among themselves a clear, consistent analysis of the play's theatrical contract.

The analysis of a play's theatrical contract has implications for all of a production's artistic collaborators: its director, actors, and designers. This chapter shows you how to approach this analysis.

Contracts vs. Conventions

It is easy to confuse our idea of the theatrical contract with the broader idea of **theatrical conventions,** or techniques shared by a majority of the plays of a period. Throughout theatre history, the plays of particular periods have exhibited ways of doing things onstage that were shared by most plays of that time. For instance, Sophocles's use of the chorus in *Antigone* is representative of ancient Greek tragedy: Aeschylus, Sophocles, and Euripides employed choruses. Likewise Shakespeare's use of the soliloquy is representative of Elizabethan and Jacobean playwrights.

A theatrical contract, by contrast, pertains only to an individual play and not to a group of plays. A playwright may choose to break from the theatrical conventions of the time; that is, a playwright may use approaches (contracts) that are unique to a specific play and that break from the conventions of the period. On the one hand, it is useful to be aware of a period's theatrical conventions; on the other hand, we must stay alert to the possibility that a play uses contracts unique to that play.

In analyzing plays for their theatrical contracts, it is helpful to think of two forms or divisions of theatrical contracts. One, **presentational** and **representational contracts,** refers to ways characters relate to the audience. The second, **realistic** and **nonrealistic contracts,** refers to the way in which production elements such as character behavior, scenery, costumes, lights, properties, sound, and language are heightened or distorted.

Play analysis involves searching the play for clues as to which kinds of contracts (presentational or representational, and realistic or nonrealistic) are being proposed. Production teams must be aware of the ways these elements are used throughout the play, because the theatrical contract can influence the shape of the designs, the ways characters relate to the audience, the development of the plot, and even the meaning of the play.

Presentational and Representational Contracts

A defining characteristic of theatre is that the audience and the characters are present in the same place at the same time. However, plays differ in the way that this shared reality is or is not acknowledged. Presentational plays contract for characters to interact occasionally with the audience; representational plays contract for their characters to ignore the audience's presence.

The first question to be asked about presentational and representational contracts is, Does any character in the play *overtly* address the audience? If the answer is yes, the contract is presentational; if the answer is no, the contract is representational.

Presentational Contracts

In a presentational contract one or more of the characters *directly address the audience*. This may take the form of **soliloquies** (in which the character is alone on stage and addresses the audience), **asides** (in which the character turns from interaction with other characters and addresses the audience as if the others cannot hear the comment), or **songs** directed at the audience. The key is that in a presentational contract one or more characters acknowledge the audience as sharing their reality in time and space, treating the audience almost as if it were another character in the play, and seeking its emotional support or intellectual agreement.

Do characters in presentational plays engage constantly in direct address? No. Except in a few rare cases, soliloquies, asides, and songs are usually interspersed into longer scenes in which the characters interact without acknowledging the audience. For purposes of our system of play analysis, however, if there is some direct address to the audience the play becomes a presentational play, because the possibility of direct address is always present.

Representational Contracts

In a representational contract, an agreement exists that the world of the play is to be treated as separate from the audience. The representational contract calls for the characters to refrain from overtly recognizing the audience's presence. Of course, the actors know the audience is present, but there is an unspoken agreement that the characters will not overtly acknowledge the audience's presence. Representational theater is characterized by the metaphor of the "fourth wall" imagined to be standing between the characters and the audience making them invisible to each other. The characters address each other, but no asides or soliloquies are addressed to the audience. The world of the play is separate from the world of the audience. In short, in a representational contract the audience is a voyeur.

Value in Understanding the Playwright's Intentions

In most of theatre history, plays were performed presentationally. The choral odes of ancient Greek dramas were written for a theatrical contract in which the audience's presence was recognized. In Aristophanes's Greek comedies, for instance, some passages are addressed to the audience; they refer to contemporary Athenian politicians and leading citizens, many of whom were in the audience, at whom Aristophanes was poking fun. Likewise, in the sixteenth-, seventeenth-, and eighteenth-century plays of Shakespeare, Molière, and Sheridan, characters recognize the audience's presence through asides and soliloquies. The three pre–

nineteenth-century plays we examine throughout this book—*Antigone, Hamlet,* and *Tartuffe*—use presentational contracts. The nineteenth, twentieth, and twenty-first centuries saw the emergence and eventual dominance of the representational contract including, plays such as Henrik Ibsen's *A Doll House,* August Strindberg's *Miss Julie,* August Wilson's *Joe Turner's Come and Gone,* and Tracy Letts's *August: Osage County.*

What is the implication of this theatre history discussion for the study of play analysis? If we are to understand a play's intended contract, we must be aware of theatre practice at the time of its original production, and how the play conforms to and departs from the norm. Such departures can reveal important information concerning the playwright's specific intentions.

Direct Address and Audience Identification

Play analysts must consider how the use of representational or presentational contracts may affect the audience's experience of the play. Can we predict? Yes, but not with absolute certainty.

Representational contracts tend to draw us in, encouraging the audience to identify with and empathize with the characters, thus diminishing the audience's objectivity or distance. When we are encouraged to view events onstage as if we were peering through a keyhole at real life events, we tend to forget ourselves, forget we are in a theatre. Perhaps this is intensified by the importance of film in today's culture. Film expertly uses representational techniques to draw us in and intensify our emotional involvement. Few commercial films use characters who address the audience directly. We are conditioned to enter into representational contracts both in film and in nonmusical theater.

In plays using presentational contracts, each time a character addresses us we seem to be reminded we are in a theatre, and as a result we may to some degree be distanced from the production. Our emotional involvement may be affected, perhaps diminished. The twentieth-century German playwright Bertolt Brecht, for instance, intentionally used songs, soliloquies, and asides to keep the audience alienated from the emotions onstage and to maintain a more objective perspective regarding the events being presented.

On the other hand, if the character who addresses us manages to charm us, to engage us positively, we may find our identification increased, enhanced. This seems natural: People develop stronger connections to those who talk to them than to those who ignore them. In everyday life, when people bring us into their confidence, we tend to identify with them, root for them. We tend to think of them being on our side, and of us being on their side. For example, Peter Shaffer's psychological drama, *Equus,* breaks occasionally from character interactions to present, in direct address, psychiatrist Martin Dysart's introspective reflections on the play's events. Dysart's comments to us increase our identification with him and with his dilemmas about psychiatric treatment.

Paradoxically, some of Shakespeare's most successful villains are characters who engage us in direct address, charming us into identifying with them and their dastardly behavior. This makes our identification problematic: We find ourselves encouraged to be on the side of a morally objectionable character and thus are made uncomfortable in our relationship to the events of the play. Iago in *Othello* and Richard in *Richard III* are good examples of such characters.

Moral problems aside, we tend to see a play's events through the eyes of the character who talks to us, and our perception will be colored by the spin the character gives events. This is certainly the case with *Hamlet*, in which the title character frequently addresses the audience and interprets events from his own perspective. However, one other character, Claudius, also briefly addresses the audience during the scene in which he is at prayer. What effect might Claudius's direct address have on a spectator's opinion of him? Why might Shakespeare have done this? Or is it possible Claudius isn't addressing the audience at all but rather is speaking to God? Such questions are important for analysis of presentational contract plays.

Once we have identified a presentational contract, and the characters who directly address the audience, the next step is to examine when the characters address the audience and in what way. Do the characters step outside the action of the play to address the audience, or do they do so from within the action? Do they use long soliloquies or short asides? For instance, in *Tartuffe*, the maid Dorine uses short comic asides to make fun of two young lovers, Mariane and Valère, who are having a childish quarrel. Other characters have similar asides, all within the flow of the action. In contrast, the chorus in *Antigone* stands outside the action and comments on the plot through long soliloquies. None of *Antigone*'s characters address the audience from within the play's action.

In summary, when we have identified a play as having a presentational contract, three central questions should be asked:

1. Who addresses the audience?
2. How might the direct address affect the way the audience experiences the character and the play?
3. When and how does the character address the audience?

Realistic and Nonrealistic Contracts

In addition to analyzing a play's use of a presentational or a representational contract, we must analyze whether a play suggests a realistic or a nonrealistic contract.

The terms *realism* and *nonrealism* refer to the degree to which *production elements* are or are not abstracted (removed to some degree) from what we think of as everyday life or everyday reality. We acknowledge that philosophers to this day continue to discuss the nature of reality; for our purposes, everyday reality consists of those aspects of life that can be objectively perceived by the senses in the normal course of daily living.

By production elements we mean every aspect of a production: language, scenery, lighting, costumes, sound, properties, movement, plot, characterization, and all other elements.

Realistic Contracts

In a realistic contract the production elements will be arranged in a manner that says, "We want to mutually agree with you, the audience, that the language, the properties, the scenery and costumes, the sound effects, the lighting, and other production elements will be presented with attention to verisimilitude (correspondence to everyday life). We know you are not deluded into thinking that the blanks we fire from our gun are real bullets, but we are trying to create a detailed appearance of reality."

A realistic contract attempts to make what we see and hear on stage resemble what we see and hear in real life. A room is designed to look like a room we might live in, the lighting resembles the kind of light we would encounter in such a room, the costumes look like clothing that might actually be worn, and people talk in ways that we might hear people speak. All elements of production are designed to approximate outward reality.

Nonrealistic Contracts

A nonrealistic contract abstracts elements from reality. **Abstraction** can be thought of as existing on a continuum from merely heightening an element to distorting an element. If an element is heightened, it is presented in such a way that some part of it is intensified. For example, in musical theatre, the songs and orchestral accompaniment often heighten or intensify emotion. On the other hand, distortion may involve an extreme removal from reality, a twisting out of shape; for example, a judge sitting at a bench several feet above the accused. The production might use a pink light to heighten the emotional effect of a song, or it might use an intense red light to distort the emotional effect.

The basic question we might ask in determining whether the play's theatrical contract is realistic or nonrealistic is: Are any of the production elements abstracted, that is, heightened or distorted in any way?

If the answer is no, the theatrical contract is realistic; if yes, the contract is nonrealistic.

Chapter 4 ■ Theatrical Contract

Identifying Abstracted Elements

The fact that a play uses elements of production that are nonrealistic does not mean that the theatrical contract calls for all elements of production to be nonrealistic. In most plays only a few elements are abstracted. After all, the actors remain real, and the introduction of total abstraction would render most plays incomprehensible.

We might say it is usual, normal, for plays to mix realistic and nonrealistic elements. Shakespeare's characters speak verse (nonrealistic language), but in most productions they do so in a world of realistic swords and chairs. In most nonrealistic contracts the production elements are arranged as if to say, "On a continuum of reality, from the realistic to the totally fantastical, we have chosen this degree of abstraction. Some elements of the play do not appear to be realistic, but we want you to agree that within the world of this production, the elements are real to the characters. All elements may not be equally abstracted. For example, we may sing and dance abstractly, but our costumes and scenery will resemble the real thing."

Most audiences readily accept mixtures in theatrical contracts in which abstract, poetic dialogue is spoken by characters who are wearing authentic period costumes, acting on a bare platform stage that is an abstracted representation of a specific locale, while dueling with authentic replica swords and daggers, and who fall dead from stab wounds that may or may not produce realistic blood. In *Equus*, the audience accepts that most of the characters are dressed in realistic clothing, while the actors playing the horses wear on their heads abstract horses' heads made of wire and on their feet aluminum cothurni that suggest hooves and are otherwise clad in black dancers' leotards. The effect of these choices is to emphasize the god-like aspect of the horses, while reflecting their near-human intelligence. The key seems to be thoughtful choices made with the audience's potential experience in mind: What will the audience members accept? What might confuse them about the contract being presented?

Plausibility vs. Nonrealism

It is important to distinguish between nonrealistic elements of a play and implausibility. Plausibility has to do with believability. For example, a character might exit to perform a task in an adjoining room and return a moment later having performed the task. That is believable; it's plausible. However, if a character exits to explore a situation occurring twenty miles away and reenters seconds later to report on it, that's unbelievable. It's implausible.

Realism and nonrealism have to do with plays creating contracts in which elements are presented with close adherence to everyday life (realism) or in which elements are abstracted (nonrealism). Shakespeare created characters who speak in formal verse; the language is abstracted, nonrealistic. Because of the play's contract, it is believable, plausible, that these characters think and speak in verse.

One production of *Hamlet* created a contract in which properties were mimed, thus treating the properties nonrealistically. Therefore, the final fight between Laertes and Hamlet involved vicious thrusts with imaginary swords. The production had created a contract using imaginary properties so that a fight with imaginary swords became plausible. It was nonrealistic but believable.

In summary, when we have identified a play as being nonrealistic, two basic questions should be asked:

1. What elements of the play are abstracted?
2. What is the apparent effect of the abstraction?

The Theatrical Contract in *The Glass Menagerie*

Questions about Direct Address

1. In *The Glass Menagerie,* who addresses the audience? Obviously you need not reread the play to answer the question: Tom addresses the audience, and no other character does.
2. At what moments does Tom address the audience? Is a pattern associated with his moments of direct address?
3. Is there any moment when Tom interrupts a scene to introduce an aside? We have said the privilege of direct address affects the audience's perspective; that is audiences tend to identify with characters who confide in them. Does Tom's perspective affect your attitudes toward Amanda? Laura? Jim? At the play's end, how do you feel about Tom's having abandoned his mother and "crippled" sister? Is this related to his having had the privilege of direct address?
4. Imagine the play with each of the four characters having the privilege of addressing you, stating a case for her or his behavior. How might that affect the way the story was perceived?
5. Would you feel differently about Tom abandoning Amanda and Laura if he hadn't had the privilege of direct address? How might you feel differently toward him? How might you feel differently about Amanda? Laura? Why?
6. A frame establishes boundaries; for example, a picture frame limits the boundary of the picture. How do Tom's moments of direct address function as frames for time? As frames for place?

Chapter 4 ■ Theatrical Contract

Questions about Abstraction and Nonrealism

There is no doubt that elements of the play are abstracted. Tom opens the play with a speech telling us how he will present the events of his home life poetically. With *The Glass Menagerie* the play analyst's task is to identify the multiple elements that are abstracted and to clarify their effects on the play.

1. Can you identify instances of characters using language abstractly? Poetically?
2. Which character's language seems most to reflect realism, the language you would expect everyday people to use? Nonrealism?
3. How do Williams's stage directions demand scenery and properties that are abstracted?
4. The projections that Williams describes in the stage directions were eliminated for the first professional production of the play. Most productions eliminate them. How would the play have a different effect on the audience with and without the projections?
5. Williams describes several lighting effects in the stage directions. What effect will they have in relation to realism and nonrealism?
6. Williams's stage directions describe the use of scrim and gauze. How might these effects make the production more or less abstract?
7. Williams's stage directions call for candlelight. What seems to be the intended effect? Could candlelight (a real phenomenon) abstract the play?
8. What sound effects does Williams call for? How might they create abstraction in the production?
9. Williams's stage directions describe the meal scene that opens the play as taking place "without food or utensils." How is this non-realistic element, introduced at the play's beginning, likely to affect the audience's reception of the play's theatrical contract?
10. Tom tells the audience this is a "memory" play and makes it clear the memories are his. However, the play has two scenes that Tom could not have observed: Amanda confronting Laura about her "deception:" and the part of the "Gentleman Caller" scene that involves only Laura and Jim. Is it possible these scenes demand special treatment because of their irregularity? Assume that Williams intended the scenes to be presented differently from the scenes Tom actually experiences. How might a production team communicate this?

Questions about the Theatrical Contract in Any Play

1. Do any characters in the play *overtly* address the audience? If so, which?
2. When do they address the audience and in what way? With soliloquies? Asides? Songs?
3. How might the audience be affected by the use of direct address?
4. Are any of the production elements abstracted, that is, heightened or distorted in any way? If so, which ones, and how are they abstracted?
5. What is the apparent effect of the abstraction?

LEVEL FOUR

Interpretation

5

Characters

Play analysts can understand a play as a whole, especially its conflict-resolution structure (see Chapter 2), by analyzing its characters and their interactions, studying what the characters do and how their mutually opposed motives create the play's conflict.

As we said in Chapter 1, play analysts must think of dialogue not as mere talk but as doing, as actions that characters take in their efforts to affect the way others think of them and treat them. Of course, stage directions may also describe characters' physical actions. Dialogue and stage directions combine to provide information about characters: who they are and what they do. Understanding characters from multiple perspectives is an essential part of play analysis.

Aspects of Characters

Existing Relationships

Analysis demands that we identify existing connections among characters: Are they social relationships? Work relationships? Religious relationships? Family relationships?

Identifying existing relationships is relatively easy in small-cast plays. But in many plays, especially those written before World War II, there can be twenty or more characters. In such cases it may be difficult to keep track of who the characters are, let alone who they are to each other. For example, characters in Russian plays may be referred to by nicknames, given names, and family names that are unfamiliar to us. And in some Shakespearean plays, characters may be spoken of both by their family names and by their various titles. In William Shakespeare's *Richard II*, for example, Bolingbrook, Lancaster, Hereford, Henry, and King Henry IV are all the same person.

One technique for keeping track of characters' relationships is to map them. This gives you a visual way to differentiate and describe the characters and their relationships to each other. Appendix 2 explains character maps and provides an example.

In addition to identifying relationships (mother, son, boss, friend, etc.), it is valuable to know the quality of the relationships at the start of the play. For example, the mother may be frustrated with the son, or the wife may be bored with the husband. This information may reveal and clarify conflicts between characters.

Let's look at the opening of Sophocles's *Antigone* and examine how we learn about an existing relationship. Remember, when an audience is watching the play for the first time (and when you are reading it for the first time), they must gather information from hints and references in the dialogue. A good playwright skillfully plants this information while advancing the plot.

When we encounter Antigone and Ismene at the beginning of the play, the dialogue tells us they are sisters who have important differences between them: Antigone is the aggressive, assertive sister, and Ismene is the passive one who accepts Creon's decree. Here is how we gather that information [our comments are in brackets]:

Ismene: ... I am no nearer knowing
Whether my luck has changed for good or bad.

Antigone: I know, too well.
[Notice the direct contrast: Ismene doesn't know, and Antigone does.]
That is why I wanted to bring you
Outside the courtyard, to talk to you alone.

Ismene: What is it? Trouble, you do not need to tell me.
[Ismene prefers to keep her head in the sand.]

Antigone: What else, when Creon singles out one brother
For a hero's grave and lets the other rot?
[Antigone ignores Ismene's attempt to hide, and roars into the situation.]

And, a few lines later:

Antigone: So there you have it. Now we shall soon find out
If you are a true-born daughter of your line,
Or if you will disgrace your noble blood!
[They come from noble ancestors.]

Ismene: But, my poor sister,
[They are sisters.]

Chapter 5 ■ Characters

> If things are as you say,
> What ways and means have I to set them straight?
> *[Again, Ismene shows her helplessness.]*

Sophocles has quickly and efficiently introduced Antigone and Ismene's existing relationship and has contrasted the sisters.

Responses to Given Circumstances

Characters differ as to what given circumstances affect them most. One character may be affected immensely by religion, whereas economics may be far more important to another. Conflict evolves, in part, out of their different responses to given circumstances.

For example, in *Antigone*, Creon and Antigone come into conflict because of the profoundly different importance they give to the state on the one hand, and religion and family on the other hand. For Creon the political situation is most important in his decision to forbid burial to Eteocles, whom Creon considers a traitor. Antigone, by contrast, puts religion and family responsibility ahead of politics when she defies Creon's order forbidding burial. These contrasting values generate the play's central conflict.

Simple vs. Complex Behavior

Another perspective from which to understand characters is to analyze whether the playwright has given them simple or complex ways of behaving toward others. In many comedies stereotypical and predictable behavior is the source of humor. For example, in Molière's *Tartuffe*, Dorine the maid is consistently impertinent (at least for a servant) with her superiors: In the first scene, Madame Pernelle tells her, "Girl, you talk too much and I'm afraid / You're far too saucy for a lady's-maid," and her assessment is right. Dorine is equally impertinent toward her master, Orgon, when he inquires about Tartuffe's welfare, and later she's disrespectful toward Orgon when he proposes to marry his daughter, Mariane, to Tartuffe. This irreverent behavior carries over even into her advice to Mariane about how to avoid marrying Tartuffe.

However, most dramatic characters are not so one dimensional. Most characters are like us and the people we know; that is, they are situational. They are complicated, irregular, inconsistent, neither always honest nor dishonest, neither always pleasant nor unpleasant, neither always direct nor indirect. In short, they are not monolithic: plain, undefined, without irregularity. A close, perceptive play reading involves both the identification of the ways characters behave predictably and the identification of the ways they are complex.

Our situational behavior is influenced by what we want from others in specific relationships. People may interact differently with persons of superior status (bosses, for example, or kings) than with persons of inferior status. They may be different with their mothers than with their fathers, different with brothers than with sisters. Consider how you behave with each of your close relatives. Consider how you interact with each of your friends.

A careful reader of *Hamlet* will notice profound differences in the way Hamlet treats others. He treats his "friends" Rosencrantz and Guildenstern differently from his friend Horatio. He treats Polonius differently from Ophelia. He treats his mother differently at the beginning of the play than after he learns how his father died, and he shifts again in how he treats her after his return from England. These changes are important information for our understanding of Hamlet.

Characters Are Tactical

It is especially important to observe tactics characters use. We define **tactics** as the strategies characters use to get what they want from others. We identified Dorine in *Tartuffe* as being rather one dimensional in her impertinence, but this does not mean that she uses the same tactics in her dealings with different people or different situations. When Dorine deals with Madame Pernelle in the first scene, for example, her tactics are confrontational. She contradicts Orgon's mother: "You see him as a saint. I'm far less awed; / In fact, I see right through him. He's a fraud." But when she deals with Orgon in Act I, Scene 3, she uses different tactics: She seems to defer to Orgon in telling him how Elmire has suffered and how well Tartuffe has been. Of course, her tactics are designed to allow the audience to observe how much more concerned Orgon is for Tartuffe than he is for his wife and children. In Act II, Scene 2, she treats Orgon's intention of marrying Mariane to Tartuffe as though it's a lie that couldn't possibly be true: "There's lately been a rumor going about— / Based on some hunch or chance remark, no doubt— / That you mean Mariane to wed Tartuffe. / I've laughed it off, of course, as just a spoof." Without confronting him directly, Dorine lets Orgon know just how silly she thinks his idea is.

Points of View

In addition to being situational, like us, dramatic characters are often egocentric; that is, they see the world in terms of themselves. We don't mean necessarily they are selfish; we mean they tend to see others from a limited perspective: their own. Part of understanding a character's behavior is to question how the character sees others. To understand Hamlet's behavior we must understand how he sees Claudius, Gertrude, Ophelia, and others.

Likewise, we learn about characters by observing how others view them. What do others say about a character? Are the comments others make about a character consistent? Or are there multiple views of the character? Comments may be made when the character described isn't present. Of course, we must question whether such behind-the-back comments are reliable; nevertheless, we must gather, interpret, and analyze information from what one character says about another. Remember, in this process of studying dialogue for information about characters, we learn both about the speaker and about the person who is described.

Stage Directions as Character Information

Stage directions tell us about characters. The modern Anglo-Irish playwright George Bernard Shaw represents an extreme of dramatists telling us about characters through stage directions; his character descriptions sometimes go on literally for pages. On the other hand, the playwrights of Athens's golden age (Aeschylus, Sophocles, and Euripides) provide almost no stage directions. Molière's seventeenth-century plays provide few stage directions. Likewise, Shakespeare's sixteenth- and seventeenth-century plays provide few stage directions, and those few that are given usually indicate entrances, exits, and occasionally sound effects.

Look at *Antigone*, *Tartuffe*, and *Hamlet*, with attention to their stage directions. Remember that most editors place brackets around the stage directions that they have added. In most editions of plays, the stage directions without brackets are those that the playwrights wrote into their original manuscripts.

In turn, look at August Wilson's stage directions for *Joe Turner's Come and Gone*, written in 1987. Do you see how much Wilson, in his stage directions, tells us about his people and their backgrounds? Comparing Wilson's stage directions with *Antigone*, *Hamlet*, and *Tartuffe* illustrates clearly the differences between modern and contemporary playwrights who often provide extensive character descriptions, and playwrights of earlier times who depend on our finding character information in the play's dialogue.

Language Informs Us about Characters

At the beginning of Act I, Scene 3, of *Joe Turner's Come and Gone*, Seth, the owner of the play's boardinghouse, is talking about his frustrations in getting two White businessmen to invest in his business idea. He says,

> Seth: They can't see that. Neither one of them can see that. Now, how much sense it take to see that? All you got to do is be able to count. One man making ten pots is five men making fifty pots. But

they can't see that. Hell, I can teach anybody how to make a pot. I can teach you. I can take you out there and get you started right now. Inside of two weeks you'd know how to make a pot. All you got to do is want to do it. I can get five men. I ain't worried about getting no five men.

From studying this speech and its language, we learn a great deal about Seth. Throughout the play we see that Seth is very much a businessman, always concerned about making money in some way. From this speech we see he is ambitious, not content to be a lone man making pots ten at a time; rather he wants to expand into a small business with five men making fifty pots. We see also that he is frustrated because he can't get White investors to see the logic of his proposition. This frustration comes through in his short, adamant sentences and the way he repeats phrases, hammering home his point. His "incorrect" grammar tells us that he is not well educated. Nevertheless, we see by the power of his ideas and by the clarity of his logic that he is an intelligent man.

Compare Seth's speech with one of Bynum's a few moments later. Bynum, a man in his early sixties, is a "conjure man," a worker of traditional African religious magic. He is talking to a young man named Jeremy, who at the moment is thinking, impulsively, of moving in with a young woman named Mattie Campbell, whom he finds attractive. Bynum says,

Bynum: All right. Let's try it this way. Now, you take a ship. Be out there on the water traveling about. You out there on that ship sailing to and from. And then you see some land. Just like you see a woman walking down the street. You see that land and it don't look like nothing but a line out there on the horizon. That's all it is when you first see it. A line that cross your path out there. He know that if you get off the water to go take a good look . . . why, there's a whole world right there. A whole world with everything imaginable under the sun. Anything you can think of you can find on that land. Same with a woman. A woman is everything a man need. To a smart man she water and berries. And that's all a man need. That's all he need to live on. You give me some water and berries, and if there ain't nothing else I can live a hundred years. See, you just like a man looking at the horizon from a ship. You just seeing a part of it. But it's a blessing when you learn to look at a woman and see in maybe just a few strands of her hair, the way her cheek curves . . . to see in that everything there is out of life to be gotten.

Bynum's language is much different from Seth's: more elaborate, metaphoric, and poetic. Unlike Seth's short, passionate sentences,

Bynum's are longer and more musical, and their content is much more philosophical. Whereas Seth is focused on business, Bynum is looking at something larger and deeper, if less practical. It is not simply *what* the two talk about but *how* they talk about it that reveals their characters.

Dialogue Suggests Characters' Physical Actions

In addition to supplying information about the speaker's interests and goals, dialogue can suggest the speaker's physical movements. Analyzing Shakespeare's plays and others like them that do not have extensive stage directions demands that we search for stage directions implied in the dialogue.

A passage in *Romeo and Juliet* illustrates how characters' movements may be embedded in the dialogue. Although it is not one of the plays from which we draw examples elsewhere in the book, it is a famous scene that many will have read or seen, and it is an example of a scene in which actors often overlook the implied stage directions. In this passage Romeo and Juliet meet and have their first conversation at a party hosted by Juliet's family and at which Romeo and his friends are uninvited guests. Juliet does not know he is a rival Montague; Romeo knows she's a Capulet. You don't need to have read the play to understand the illustration; rather, pay careful attention to the process we are illustrating. Brackets indicate our implied stage directions; the line numbers are ours, not Shakespeare's.

Romeo: 1 If I profane with my unworthiest hand,
2 This holy shrine, the gentle sin is this,
[The "holy shrine" refers to her hand.]
3 My lips two blushing Pilgrims ready stand,
[At some point in the first three lines, Romeo takes her hand in his.]
4 To smooth that rough touch, with a tender kiss.
[This implies he'll kiss her hand.]

Juliet: 5 Good Pilgrim, you do wrong your hand too much,
6 Which mannerly devotion shows in this,
7 For Saints have hands that Pilgrims hands do touch,
8 And palm to palm, is holy Palmers kiss.
[Juliet's speech implies that she has withdrawn her hand from being kissed. She offers her palm, facing out, to Romeo, suggesting they kiss the way the Palmers did, by touching hand to hand, "palm to palm." Palmers were persons who made pilgrimages to Jerusalem during the Crusades, stopping along the road to venerate statues of saints and kiss the statues' hands.]

Romeo: 9 Have not Saints lips and holy Palmers too?
[He's returning her verbal image: both saints and Palmers have lips.]

Juliet: **10** Aye Pilgrim, lips that they must use in prayer.
[She deflects his offer to kiss her.]

Romeo: **11** O then dear Saint, let lips do what hands do,
12 They pray (grant thou) least faith turn to despair.
[He picks up on the image of her being a saint and suggests that she let his lips kiss hers in the way that Pilgrims' hands kiss.]

Juliet: **13** Saints do not move, though grant for prayers sake.
[She implies that the saints are statues that don't move but that they are responsive to prayer. In other words, "I won't move in to kiss you, but I'll stand still like a saint while you kiss me."]

Romeo: **14** Then move not while my prayers effect I take:
[He's saying, if she'll stand still he'll move in and kiss her.]
[The script has no stage direction for a kiss, but between lines 14 and 15 a kiss takes place. How do we know? Because he refers in line 15 to his lips having been purged of sin by kissing hers.]
15 Thus from my lips, by thine my sin is purg'd.

Juliet: **16** Then have my lips the sin that they have took.

Romeo: **17** Sin from my lips? O trespass sweetly urg'd:
18 Give me my sin again.
[He's asking for another kiss.]

Juliet: You kiss by th' booke.
[He must have kissed her. Clearly she's commenting on his kiss.]

Few passages of dramatic dialogue are so laden with implied stage directions. In addition to demonstrating the need to mine implied stage directions from dialogue, the passage also informs us about the characters. We learn from the dialogue that both Juliet and Romeo are extremely bright; they are persons who are able to be witty while being romantic. In fact, they have spoken in the form of a sonnet with every-other-line rhyming, a considerable achievement.

Characters Evoke Conflict, and Conflict Reveals Character

Dramatic action depends on conflict: If there is no conflict, there is no drama. And for there to be conflict, two or more characters must have mutually opposed wants, desires, or needs. In other words, conflict emerges from opposition.

To understand a play's conflict, we explore characters in terms of what they are seeking that puts them in opposition to others. That is, what goals and tactics do opposing characters pursue? By answering these questions about goals and tactics, we reveal the central sources of a play's conflict. And by understanding characters in relationship to conflict, we understand the characters' functions in the play. What are their goals in relation to the other people in the play? What tactics do they use to get what they want?

Sometimes that conflict may be subtle. The *Romeo and Juliet* scene we studied for its stage directions in the dialogue may seem initially to have little conflict. After all, the characters seem attracted to each other and want to kiss. But there is conflict: conflict over how soon and under what conditions they will kiss. Romeo offers to kiss Juliet early in the scene, but Juliet, perhaps because it would be unseemly to be persuaded quickly, makes Romeo woo her through an elaborate verbal game. This stimulates Romeo to alter his language. He changes his tactic from a direct offer to kiss her hand, which seems somehow rather brash, to a metaphorical exchange that draws a parallel between Juliet and a saint—a much more romantic approach than his first. The potential for rejection creates tension in most of us. Actors who find ways to be attracted to their Romeo or Juliet will locate this scene's tension and conflict.

At other times the conflict between characters will be more obvious and more apparently intense. At these moments, characters may reveal their most essential values. For example, is it more important for the character to be right and win an argument? Or is she willing to lose the argument and win the young man? Through the analysis of such decisions, we learn about the character's essential values.

Characters in *The Glass Menagerie*

Questions about the Characters' Existing Relationships

Because *The Glass Menagerie* has so few characters, there is a temptation not to bother with formally asking questions about the characters' existing relationships. But even with this small-cast play, you must ask an essential question: What are the existing relationships among the characters at the beginning of the play?

Tom's opening monologue tells who the family members are, but additional questions must be asked. Starting with the first scene, what do you learn about the existing relationships among the three family members?

1. How is Amanda dissatisfied with Tom?
2. How is Amanda trying to change Laura's behavior?
3. Does either Tom or Laura rebel against Amanda's authority?
4. What do you learn about Tom and Laura's relationship to Amanda from the following exchange?

Tom: I know what's coming!
Laura: Yes. But let her tell it.
Tom: Again?
Laura: She loves to tell it.

Questions about Responses to Given Circumstances

Especially through his monologues, Tom demonstrates a keen awareness of conditions and events outside the Wingfield home: international events, economic conditions, the popularity of movies, and the place of movies in his life and in the culture.

1. Does any other character demonstrate this level of awareness and concern for the outside world?
2. Is there a difference between Tom's outside world concerns during his monologues and his outside world concerns during the dialogue scenes with Amanda, Laura, and Jim?
3. How might you compare Tom's and Jim's concerns for the outside world?

   Note that Jim asks for the sports section of the paper and comments on Dizzy Dean's antics. Jim attended the Century of Progress exposition. In his conversation with Laura, Jim demonstrates awareness of popular psychology and he shows a desire to improve himself economically. We might say, figuratively, that Tom's awareness of Berchtesgaden and Jim's interest in Dizzy Dean and the sports page help define how they relate differently to the outside world. On the other hand, Tom's awareness of the outside world is demonstrated mainly in his monologues. In dialogue scenes he seems more aware of poets and movies. What might you make of that?

4. Is it possible that Tom, during the dialogue scenes, is immensely egocentric, seeing the world only as it affects his immediate concerns? And is it possible that the Tom of the monologues is a more mature and less egocentric person?
5. How are Amanda's interests in events outside the home different from Tom's? Clearly she is affected by the Depression economy. Does she refer to economic matters differently from Tom?
6. Does Laura demonstrate interest in the world outside her home and family life? Or are her interests totally oriented to life in her home? Does she demonstrate awareness of religious, economic, and social conditions outside her home?

Questions about Race, Ethnicity, and Religion

Reading the play in a contemporary context, you may be startled by the first scene's reference to African Americans. Amanda says, "No, sister, no, sister—you be the lady this time and I'll be the darky."

1. Do the characters demonstrate elsewhere in the play the period's unself-conscious assumption of White superiority?
2. Tom tells Amanda that the gentleman caller's name is Jim O'Connor. What do you learn about Amanda from her reaction to his name?
3. Does either Tom or Laura demonstrate awareness of ethnicity or religion as an important given circumstance? Does Jim?
4. Amanda identifies Jim as being "Catholic," that is, Roman Catholic. Jim, in turn, refers to his religion in his conversation with Laura. Is there evidence of Amanda being religious? Is there evidence of either Tom or Laura being religious?

Questions about Laura's Disability

1. Laura's disability is one of the play's most important given circumstances. How do the characters react differently to Laura's disability?
2. Laura refers to herself as being "crippled." With Jim, she talks about the impact of her disability during her high school years. How important was and is her disability to her self-image?
3. What do you learn about Amanda, Tom, and Jim by examining the differences among their reactions? For example, in Scene 5, Amanda and Tom talk about Laura's disability. In another scene, Amanda rebels against Tom's use of the term *crippled*. Tom confronts Amanda with the differences between Laura and other girls. What do we learn about Laura, Amanda, and Tom from these exchanges?

Questions about Situational Behaviors

1. Jim interacts with each member of the Wingfield family. How does he treat each differently?
2. How does he confront Tom with problems at the warehouse?
3. How does he treat Amanda differently from the way Tom and Laura treat her? He is a gentleman caller. Does he bring out in Amanda the behavior of her youth?
4. Are you surprised in any way by Jim's tactics when interacting with Laura?
5. Sometimes students react to characters' situational behavior as dishonesty. Is Jim dishonest with any family member? How can you determine whether he is being honest in his treatment of Laura?

6. How does Laura demonstrate being situational in her treatment of her mother and her brother?
7. Tom is confrontational at times with Amanda. Does he ever treat Laura in a confrontational manner?
8. Do you see Amanda using confrontational tactics in some situations? For example, does she confront Tom about his eating habits? His drinking? How does she use different tactics with Tom in her effort to get him to deliver a gentleman caller for Laura?

Questions about the Relationship between Language and Goals and Tactics

1. How is Tom's language in his monologues to the audience different from his language in the dialogue scenes? If it is different, is it different because of the character with whom he's interacting? Does he talk to the audience differently from the way he talks to Amanda? Laura? Jim? How much of the difference comes from his being older in the monologues?
2. Amanda's phone calls provide another opportunity to observe a character interacting in substantially different relationships. What do you learn about Amanda from studying the language of her phone conversations? That is, how is her language different when she's talking on the telephone to persons outside the home?
3. What can you learn about each character from studying his or her language in different relationships and situations?

Question about Thought Process

1. Study Jim's thought process as he moves from saying he's "comfortable as a cow" to offering Laura chewing gum, through his telling her about the Wrigley Building, through his describing the Century of Progress exhibit. What thought process does he follow?

Questions about the Moment of Greatest Conflict

1. When Jim arrives at the Wingfield's home, Laura refuses at first to meet him at the door. When she finally greets him, her hand is so cold that he comments on it. When she's called to dinner, she faints. What do you learn about Laura from studying her behavior in two moments of intense conflict?
2. Study the moment when Laura realizes that, despite Jim's kiss, she will not be able to continue the relationship. How does she behave toward him? Toward her mother and her brother after Jim leaves?

Questions about Characters in Any Play

1. Who are the major characters?
2. What are the existing relationships among the characters: Are there social relationships? Work relationships? Religious relationships? Family relationships?
3. Create a character map (see Appendix 2).
4. What are the qualities of these relationships at the start of the play?
5. What given circumstances affect each character most?
6. Which characters are simple? Which are complex?
7. How do characters behave differently with different people?
8. What does each character say about himself or herself? What does he or she say about others?
9. What do other characters say about each character?
10. What do you learn about the characters from stage directions?
11. What does the way each character uses language tell you about his or her personality? Level of education?
12. What can you learn about each character from studying his or her language in different relationships and situations?
13. How does each character's use of language reflect his or her thought process?
14. What goals and tactics do opposing characters pursue?
15. What do you learn about the characters from their moments of greatest conflict?

6

Conflict Analysis Applied to a Scene

Just as conflict analysis is central to understanding plays as a whole, it is also integral to understanding a play's individual scenes. In fact, we can use the same terms of analysis in analyzing a scene's conflict. Scenes may be thought of as short plays in themselves, complete with a central conflict, protagonists and opposing forces (these need not be the same protagonist and opposing forces of the play as a whole), a climax, an introductory incident, a moment of engagement, and a denouement. Understanding the conflict-resolution structure of each scene has the same effect as understanding the play as a whole: It provides a sense of purpose, focus, and structure, and helps identify those moments that further the play's overall conflict.

In this chapter we apply conflict analysis to a scene from *The Glass Menagerie*. We then examine smaller units of conflict—actions and beats—and how they relate to the scene's overall conflict.

The Scene as a Unit of Conflict

What is a scene? Dictionaries and theatre textbooks offer various definitions, all of which can be useful depending on the play being examined. One concept is the French Scene: In classic French plays, when a character enters or when one exits, a new scene begins or ends. Most editions of Molière's *Tartuffe* do this. For example, in Act IV, Scene 3, Orgon, Elmire, Mariane, Cléante, and Dorine are onstage. But at the scene's end Elmire asks all but Orgon to leave: "Please leave us for a bit." Then Scene 4 begins with only Elmire and Orgon on stage. A new scene begins with the arrival of Tartuffe. Few contemporary plays use the French Scene concept, although it can be a useful way for the play analyst to begin the process of breaking down a play into smaller units.

Other definitions determine scene breaks according to changes in location or time: A scene is the action that takes place in one location continuously or that takes place continuously over an unbroken period of time; in this case, when the location or time changes, the scene changes. Many modern realistic plays use one or both of these approaches.

William Shakespeare's plays, in their original printings, had no scene divisions. Most of his editors identify scenes as ending when all characters have vacated the stage. When all the characters have exited, the scene ends; and when one or more characters enter, the next scene begins. *Hamlet* opens with Barnardo and Francisco on stage; Horatio and Marcellus enter, and then the Ghost enters and exits twice. The scene ends when Barnardo, Francisco, Horatio, and Marcellus leave, creating an empty stage. The next scene begins with the entrance of new characters.

Given these variations on the term *scene*, we might say that each play creates its own contract regarding scenes. Nevertheless, for the purposes of our approach to play analysis, which emphasizes conflict, we must create a less mechanical, more organic approach that reflects this orientation. For our purposes, then, let's say that a **scene** is a unit of conflict that has a beginning, a middle, and an end. Breaking down the play into smaller complete units of conflict allows us to apply to a scene the same terms of conflict analysis that we applied in Chapter 2 when we studied a play's overall conflict, and with equal benefits.

As in Chapter 2, we will be somewhat directive in identifying our model scene's various parts.

Conflict Analysis Applied to Scene 2 of *The Glass Menagerie*

Scene 2 is sometimes called the "deception" scene. It begins with Laura onstage alone, washing and polishing her menagerie, and its final line is Amanda's "One thing your father had *plenty* of—was *charm!* [*Tom motions to the fiddle in the wings.*] [*The scene fades out with music.*]."

We recommend that you first reread the scene, treating it as a short play in itself and applying the terms of conflict analysis introduced in Chapter 2; then read our analysis below.

Question about the Climax

1. At what moment does Scene 2 resolve its conflict? What is its moment of climax?

Chapter 6 ■ Conflict Analysis Applied to a Scene

The conflict grows out of Laura and Amanda arguing over Laura's "deception" and evolves into Amanda worrying aloud over whether Laura will marry. Amanda doesn't want Laura to become a "barely tolerated" spinster, the kind of "pitiful case" Amanda saw in the South of her youth.

Amanda moves from confronting Laura about her "deception" to wondering aloud what can be done. Then she settles on a solution: Laura must marry! The scene's climax relates to this solution: marriage for Laura. "Girls that aren't cut out for business careers usually wind up married to some nice man. *[Gets up with a spark of revival.]* Sister, that's what you'll do!" This speech resolves the conflict over Laura's future: a direction has been set and plans set in motion. It seems like the climax.

The only other moment that could contain the climax is Amanda's:

> Amanda: Nonsense! Laura, I've told you never, never to use that word. Why, you're not crippled, you just have a little defect—hardly noticeable, even! When people have some slight disadvantage like that, they cultivate other things to make up for it—develop charm—and vivacity—and—charm! That's all you have to do *[She turns again to the photograph.]* One thing your father had *plenty* of—was *charm!*

However, this speech resolves no conflict; it merely recommends a strategy: cultivate charm. Let's say the scene's climax is the one we suggested earlier: "Girls that aren't cut out for business careers usually wind up married to some nice man. *[Gets up with a spark of revival.]* Sister, that's what you'll do!" The conflict is resolved; at least it's resolved for Amanda, who is driving this scene: Laura will marry.

Questions about the Major Dramatic Question

1. What major dramatic question is answered in the scene's moment of climax?

   Perhaps it is, Will Amanda find a course of action to assure that Laura will have a secure future?

2. Does this question seem to apply to the scene as a whole? Can it be used as the Protagonist's main objective?

   Yes. At the beginning of the scene, Amanda focused on the debacle at the business school; but that topic evolved into a larger concern: Amanda's determination that Laura have a secure future. Amanda's questions about the boy at school represent more than idle curiosity; they are the beginning of a thought process and a direction that she drives toward with increasing focus: getting Laura to understand that her future must be ensured through marriage. The major dramatic question can be converted to "Amanda wants to find a course of action to assure that Laura will have a secure future." Obviously you may choose alternative phrasing for the question.

Question about the Protagonist

1. Who drives the scene's conflict? Who makes the conflict happen?

    There are only two characters in the scene, and Laura never insists that the discussion of her future, her dependence or independence, or her possible marriage continue. So the protagonist must be Amanda. But we should not reach this conclusion merely because Amanda is our choice for the play's protagonist. There may be scenes in a play in which the play's protagonist is not the scene's protagonist or is even in the scene at all.

Question about the Opposing Forces

1. Who is the opposing force?

    If Amanda is the protagonist, the choice is easy: Laura opposes Amanda. Amanda is seeking to ensure Laura's future, seeking for Laura to be an adult, a worker, and, finally, a wife. All this is more than Laura can cope with; in her fear of coping with the world outside her home, she vomited on the floor at business school. Laura wants to stay in her home, playing her records, dusting and arranging her glass menagerie. She is the obstacle to Amanda's goals.

Question about the Introductory Incident

Having determined the scene's climax, major dramatic question, protagonist, and opposing forces, we can address earlier moments in the scene's conflict-resolution structure.

1. At what moment is the subject of the scene's conflict introduced?

    Early in the scene, before the discussion of Amanda's discoveries at Rubicam's Business College, and before the discussion of the specifics of Laura's "deception," Amanda says, "What are we going to do, what is going to become of us, what is the future?" This seems to be the introductory incident. It introduces Amanda's concern for the future (the subject of our major dramatic question), and it comes early in the scene. In the same way that it is ideal for a play's conflict to begin early, the earlier the introductory incident comes in the scene, the earlier it can be continuously dramatic (full

Chapter 6 ■ Conflict Analysis Applied to a Scene

of conflict from beginning to end). We can be encouraged: We've identified an early introductory incident that relates directly to our major dramatic question.

Question about the Moment of Engagement

We said in Chapter 2 that the moment of engagement is the point when the protagonist commits to achieving his goals. From this moment on, the protagonist struggles to overcome all opposing forces.

1. At what moment in the scene does Amanda commit to finding a solution for Laura's future?

Could the moment we identified as the scene's introductory incident also serve as its moment of engagement? In other words, could Amanda's "What are we going to do, what is going to become of us, what is the future?" serve both as introductory incident and as moment of engagement? Perhaps, but this moment seems too general; it introduces the subject, but it identifies no commitment on Amanda's part.

Rather, the moment of Amanda's commitment seems to come somewhere in the following speech:

> Amanda: [Hopelessly fingering the huge pocketbook.]
> So what are we going to do the rest of our lives? Stay home and watch the parades go by? Amuse ourselves with the glass menagerie, darling? Eternally play those worn-out phonograph records your father left as a painful reminder of him? We won't have a business career—we've given that up because it gave us nervous indigestion! [Laughs wearily.]
> What is there left but dependency all our lives? I know so well what becomes of unmarried women who aren't prepared to occupy a position. I've seen such pitiful cases in the South—barely tolerated spinsters living upon the grudging patronage of sister's husband or brother's wife!—stuck away in some little mousetrap of a room—encouraged by one in-law to visit another—little birdlike women without any nest—eating the crust of humility all their life! Is that the future that we've mapped out for ourselves? I swear it's the only alternative I can think of! Of course—some girls *do marry*.
> [Laura twists her hands nervously.]
> Haven't you ever liked some boy?

Somewhere in this speech, somewhere in Amanda's associative process, she seems to reach a conclusion, a decision; she seems to commit to finding a solution for Laura. Where is it? Remember:

There must be a sense of the future in the moment of engagement. For most of this speech Amanda is describing the worst-case scenario for Laura's future. There is a sense of despair, a sense of being at a loss. Her questions are rhetorical, not meant to be answered; rather, they paint a bleak verbal picture of a possible future. She seems to reach an impasse: "Is that the future that we've mapped out for ourselves? I swear it's the only alternative I can think of!" But suddenly she thinks of an alternative: "Of course—some girls *do marry.*" Laura has failed to acquire the skills to support herself. So, someone else, a husband, must support Laura. Given what we have identified as the scene's climax, this moment ("Of course—some girls *do marry.*") seems to be the moment in the scene when Amanda commits to seeking marriage for Laura. It is our moment of engagement.

Question about the Denouement

1. Are there moments after the scene's climax that serve as denouement?

   Yes. There are speeches in which Amanda dismisses Laura's protestations that she is "crippled." Amanda has made a decision, and nothing is going to stand in her way.

Smaller Units: Actions and Beats

To repeat our axiom: Conflict grows out of mutually opposing motives. Characters pursue overriding goals throughout the play, and those goals are in conflict. Constantin Stanislavsky called these overriding goals "super objectives." For example, Antigone seeks "to honor my brother by burying him." Creon struggles "to protect my dignity and the state's honor." Tartuffe is a religious hypocrite who wants "to possess everything Orgon has." Orgon seeks "to control everyone and everything." Orgon's wife, Elmire, struggles "to keep the family order." These characters' mutually opposed motives create the play's conflict.

Characters' motives in a scene relate to their long-term desires. But characters live moment to moment. They don't live in a state of constantly seeking to fulfill their super objectives. In analyzing a scene, it's useful, especially to actors and directors, to explore how characters' motives can be broken down into smaller units.

The terms action and beat, coined by Stanislavsky, are used inconsistently, even contradictorily, by many. However, the basic ideas can be useful in clarifying a scene's conflict. We use **action** to describe *a character's main intent in a scene.* We use **beat** to describe *a smaller, more momentary unit of intent.* Each smaller unit is whole and complete in itself but is also contained in the larger unit, much like a letter of the alphabet is complete in itself but is also part of a word, which in turn is part of a sentence. A beat is whole and complete in itself but is part of an action, which is part of the conflict-resolution structure for the play as a whole.

We phrase actions and beats as verbs, stated in the infinitive: "to [verb]." And we try to coin actions and beats so that they spark conflict in an imaginative, exciting fashion.

In Act III, Scene 3, of *Tartuffe,* Tartuffe's *action* in the scene is to seduce Elmire; hers is to dissuade Tartuffe from marrying Mariane. Elmire is the scene's protagonist; she begins the scene with a clear intention and pursues it throughout. Tartuffe is the opposing force.

Tartuffe's initial beat is "to endear myself to Elmire"; hers is "to get down to business." Tartuffe's next beat is "to warm her sexually" (he fondles her); Elmire's opposing beat is "to fend off his advances." And so it goes throughout the scene.

Actors and directors sometimes use the phrase "to be in action." For a character to be in action is for the character to be involved in conflict, to be trying to get another character to give him what he wants. For this reason, a character's overriding goal in a scene is called his action. A character's moment-to-moment units of objective are his beats.

Actions and Beats in *The Glass Menagerie*

Let's propose that Amanda's through line of motive in the play is "to secure Laura's future." Laura, on the other hand, wants "to find peace"; she can't cope with the outside world's stresses. She wants peace between Tom and Amanda; she even tells Jim about her menagerie's animals getting along with each other. Tom wants "to free myself." Jim seeks "to be admired the way I was in high school." These motives oppose each other, creating conflict.

In Scene 2 we might say Amanda's action is "to get Laura to attend to her future." During Scene 2 Amanda's action takes her through a series of beats.

The first beat is "to confront Laura with her deception." Her next beat is "to find out why?" Then, she tries "to bring Laura to her senses." Finally, she determines "to convince Laura to marry."

But the scene can be dramatic only if there are mutually opposing motives. Laura's needs must conflict with Amanda's. Amanda's action throughout the scene is "to get Laura to attend to her future." Laura seeks desperately "to get Mother to leave me at peace."

Questions on the Conflict-Resolution Structure in Any Scene

1. What is the moment when the scene's major conflict is resolved (what is its climax)?
2. What question is resolved in the moment of climax (what is the major dramatic question)?
3. Who is the person who drives the scene through its conflict-resolution process (the protagonist)?
4. Who are the opposing forces against whom the protagonist struggles?
5. What is the introductory incident (the moment in the scene when the subject of the conflict is introduced)?
6. What is the moment of engagement (the moment when the protagonist commits to resolving the scene's conflict)?
7. What part of the scene functions as denouement (the moments after the climax)?

To understand the scene's conflict from moment to moment, we study the character's action, i.e., the primary goal for the scene.

1. What is the protagonist's major need, his action?
2. And how does an opposing character's action create the scene's conflict?
3. In turn, we study the smaller units of conflict.
4. What are the beats the protagonist pursues?
5. What beats does the opposing character pursue that create and sustain conflict?

7

Supplemental Research

In earlier chapters we suggested that you would need to research a play's unfamiliar references. We said you must understand thoroughly the play's given circumstances: its specific time and place (especially when it's an historical period through which you haven't lived) and the environments that affect the characters such as social systems, cultural norms, attitudes regarding ethnicity, and attitudes toward marriage, family, and the sexes. In this chapter we discuss additional research that can help in play analysis.

We placed this chapter near the end of the book because we feel that the type of research we describe here is best done after you have completed your own analysis of the play but before you bring it together into a final synthesis. Why? Because it is important for you to do your own analysis of the play and have a firm grounding in its specifics before you encounter the ideas and interpretations of others, especially others who are "authorities." This helps ensure that others don't unduly influence you. And it helps ensure that you are creating an analysis that reflects today's culture and world view rather than an analysis that reflects another culture and time. You are reading and analyzing the play for your audience in its time and place. Historical perspectives on the play, previous productions, even the playwright's ideas reflect another time, another place, and another audience.

We call this type of research supplemental because it is research that should add to your knowledge and understanding of the play. It is not a substitute for your own analysis and creativity, nor should you be overly influenced by what you encounter during this part of your analysis. Think of supplementary research as being similar to the spices that you add to a meal to enhance its flavor: The spices are not the meal itself nor are they the starting point for the meal. You wouldn't say, "Hmmmm. What would be good with rosemary?" Rather, you would say, "What spice might make this chicken taste better?" The same is true with supplemental research: It should add spice to your analysis.

Types of Supplemental Research

Several types of supplemental research can be useful. We examine some here and give examples of how they might be used.

Biographical and Autobiographical Materials

Many playwrights and theatre artists have written autobiographies that include valuable information about the ideas and sources that informed their work. These can be especially useful if the play being studied has a strong autobiographical flavor, as is the case with *The Glass Menagerie*. It has generally been acknowledged by Tennessee Williams that *The Glass Menagerie* is his thinly disguised account of his own family and himself when he was a young man living in St. Louis in the 1930s. An examination of his *Memoirs*, therefore, could provide valuable details about a variety of things, including the apartment and neighborhood where he set the play, the general culture of St. Louis at that time, and even insights into the personalities and feelings of the people on whom the characters are based.[1] Be careful, however, that you do not accept this and other information uncritically: A play, even an autobiographical one, is still fiction. It's your job to analyze the play, as written, not to demonstrate your homework for the audience.

Interviews with artists who participated in the premiere of a play may provide insights. They can suggest, among other things, solutions to problems within the play, ideas for staging or designing, and descriptions of the approaches they took to scenes and moments. As always, regard this information as mere possibilities, and examine them in relation to your own analysis, especially your conflict analysis.

Autobiographies of directors, designers, or actors who have wrestled with the play may provide ideas. Actor, playwright, and director Steven Berkoff, for instance, wrote a fascinating book entitled *I Am Hamlet*, in which he describes what went through his mind while he was playing Hamlet in a production he also directed in 1979–1980.[2] Berkoff proceeds scene by scene, analyzing moments and describing his thought process and approach to acting. It is a fascinating demonstration of the actor's art, and he gives a multitude of insights into the play itself. South African actor Anthony Sher wrote a book entitled *The Year of the King: An Actor's Diary and Sketchbook*, in which he describes his preparation and rehearsal process for playing the title role in William Shakespeare's *Richard III*.[3] Many actors and directors have devoted portions of their autobiographies to descriptions of roles they played or productions they directed.

These accounts can offer insights into how a role might be played or how moments might be staged. There is no shame involved in "borrowing" ideas from other artists, as long as those ideas fit within the framework of your analysis.

Biographies can be equally helpful but in a slightly different way. Biographies often have a more objective viewpoint and provide historical perspective. Although they may not include the personal revelations and feelings that an autobiography often provides, they usually include a more balanced, sometimes even critical, portrait of the subject. Biographers may provide contexts their subjects may not have understood, and they may have access to information unavailable to their subjects. For instance, in *The World of Tennessee Williams*, Richard F. Leavitt reproduces a photograph of the inside of the International Shoe Company, which might provide a powerful image to be shared by the actors playing Tom and the gentleman caller.[4] In addition, the book describes one of the Williams family's apartments in St. Louis.

Some historical subjects' personal journals and letters have been published posthumously. Unlike biographies, which strive for objectivity, and autobiographies, which have the benefit of hindsight, journals and letters are records of events written at the time they occurred. They can provide a sense of immediacy as well as a strong flavor of the artist's personality and thoughts. Such documents can be less self-serving than autobiographies, because they may not have been written with an audience in mind. Actor William Redfield, for example, in letters originally written to Robert Mills between January and August 1964, describes rehearsals for Richard Burton's famed *Hamlet* directed by John Gielgud.[5] Athol Fugard published his *Notebooks: 1960–1977*, in which he describes the background for several of his plays, as well as his process of writing and producing them.[6]

The key to using such material is to avoid falling into the trap of equating the artist with the work of art. Always weigh carefully the value of the biographical information in relation to the world of the play itself, and use only that which enhances and supports your analysis.

Interviews

The published interview is a relatively recent form of journalism. There is no such thing as an interview with Sophocles, for instance, or Shakespeare, or Molière. But interviews with theatre artists, especially playwrights, can reveal useful information, including what the interview subjects had in mind when they wrote the scripts, their reactions to productions of their work, and their ideas about the thematic structure of a particular play or group of plays. For instance, in David Savran's book of interviews, *In Their Own Words: Contemporary American Playwrights*, August Wilson discusses the process of rewriting *Joe Turner's Come and Gone* during rehearsal. He says, "people had been saying before rehearsals that we should see Loomis find his song. After a read-through I knew that moment was missing. We went into rehearsal and it remained an unsolved problem. Then I came up with the idea of ending the first act with him on the floor unable to stand up. When he stands at the end, you can read that as him finding his song."[7]

Although your analysis of *Joe Turner* may have identified the importance and meaning of this moment, you might have overlooked this nuance. Such a statement by the playwright should send you back to your analysis to examine whether there is textual support for this idea and whether it fits into your view of the play. Do not, however, accept the playwright's words as gospel. Many, many playwrights have had one intention in mind and ended up writing a play that does not support that intention. There are also plays, such as Williams's *Cat on a Hot Tin Roof*, that the playwright altered on the advice of others, only to later repudiate those changes. If you are using the altered text as the basis for your production, the playwright's repudiation is not particularly helpful, because you must work with the play as it is written. Nevertheless, the playwright's reason for rejecting the changes may be helpful in understanding the play as it is published.

Past Productions

If you are working on a play that has been performed before, records of past productions may be useful to your preparation. These records might include newspaper and magazine reviews, production photographs, and video and audio recordings of the production. Keep in mind that these are records of a specific production done by particular actors, directors, and designers for a specific audience at one point in time. An approach that worked once, under different circumstances, may not work now for you.

Video recordings offer the fullest record of a production, allowing you to see an entire interpretation moment by moment. However, although it may seem at first as if you are seeing an objective document of a production, the process of putting the play on video may distort the performance in many ways. The use of multiple camera angles or close ups, for example, may provide a distorted experience of the production. Even the sound of recorded audience response may affect your perspective on the production. Nevertheless, a video production can be very useful.

Audio recordings, the only option for many older productions, can give insights into how lines might be interpreted or how roles might be played (at least vocally).

Production photos can be interesting for design elements and for staging specific scenes. You must determine whether the photographs were taken during the course of a performance or whether they were staged separately. The former may give you a sense of the play in the moment, whereas the latter may provide a distillation of a moment, one that never actually appeared onstage in the production. Both types of photos are useful in different ways.

Newspaper and magazine reviews are one step removed from videotape, audiotape, or production photos, in the sense that reviews represent experience filtered through the sensibilities of the critic. Nevertheless, critical descriptions of productions provide a sense of how a production affected a member of the audience and how specific moments or roles may have been played. Descriptive skill varies among critics, but reviewers like Kenneth Tynan or Walter Kerr, to choose famous and talented examples, can give a clear picture of a performance and production. Obviously, for productions prior to the advent of videotape, audiotape, or even photography, reviews may be the only extant record of a production.

Literary Criticism

Literary criticism can be your most fruitful, as well as the most dangerous, source of supplemental research. It can inspire new ideas, but it can also saddle productions with interpretations that are ultimately unproducible on a stage. This form of supplemental research, therefore, should be explored with an especially wary eye. Nevertheless, it can be extremely valuable in offering new insights.

Literary criticism provided the inspiration for some of the twentieth century's most famous productions. Peter Brook's existential production of Shakespeare's *King Lear*, with Paul Scofield in the title role, was inspired by Polish-born critic Jan Kott's book *Shakespeare Our Contemporary*. Laurence Olivier's Oedipal version of *Hamlet* was influenced by Sigmund Freud's interpretation of the play.

Literary criticism can take many different forms. If a play is well known you may find essays or even entire books that offer interpretations of the work. In *The Meanings of Hamlet: Modes of Literary Interpretation since Bradley*, for example, Renaissance scholar Paul Gottschalk examines more than a dozen critical interpretations of *Hamlet* and even devotes an appendix to the issue of "doubting the ghost" and another to the "closet scene."[8] You may also find works devoted to the plays of specific playwrights or to an epoch in theatre history. For instance, *Understanding August Wilson*, by Mary L. Bogumil, devotes a chapter to each of Wilson's plays written prior to 1999 and includes a chapter that examines Wilson as an African American playwright.[9]

Although you will be most interested in the material concerning the play you're analyzing, examining other plays written by the same playwright can provide insights into stylistic and thematic characteristics that appear regularly in the writer's work. The way a play fits within the conventions and attitudes of its time can add to our understanding. *Producible Interpretation: Eight English Plays, 1675–1707*, by Judith Milhous and

Robert Hume, for instance, does an outstanding job of examining the effects of different interpretive choices on a group of plays written during the English Restoration.[10] Other resources might examine the problems of a dramatic style or movement (for instance, melodrama or expressionism). Individual essays on all of these topics also can be found in a variety of theatre and literary journals such as *Modern Drama* or *Theatre Journal.*

The goal of literary critics is to make a case for their own views of plays, playwrights, and styles; consequently, their interpretations can be persuasive. Subtle themes can be brilliantly explicated, images and word usages analyzed with great erudition, and hidden meanings brought to light. Although these interpretations may be valuable to supplement your understanding, the interpretation of a play for production demands that analysts focus intently on conflict and character, contract and given circumstances. Ask yourself as you are reading an essay, Can these ideas be embodied on a stage, and can an audience member be expected to be aware of them? In addition, you should ask, Does this interpretation fit into the information I have uncovered as a result of my own analysis? If you maintain this sort of careful questioning, then literary criticism can be an important source of inspiration.

Theatrical Conditions

It can be especially helpful to study theatrical practices that existed when the play was first produced. This is particularly true of plays written for historical periods and for cultures far removed from your own. The farther away a play is from your own experience, the more important it is to understand clearly what conventions served as its foundation. Peter D. Arnott's *Public and Performance in the Greek Theatre,* for instance, examines classical Greek plays in terms of each element of production (audience, chorus, actors, costume, and speech) and places them within the context of classical Greek society and of Greek theatre practice in general.[11] Arnott even examines the impact of theatre architecture on the structure of the plays. Such information can be especially helpful in understanding elements of the theatrical contract, for example, or the author's use of language or spectacle.

A Note on the Internet

The Internet can be a valuable tool in conducting supplemental research. A considerable amount of information is available on the Internet that cannot be found anywhere else. But we offer a note of caution: Although the Internet makes a great deal of information available, much of it is amateurish and unsupported by facts. You can be confident that essays in a professional journal, or information in a book from a major publisher, went through a review process that ensures a certain level of quality and knowledge, but the Internet is indiscriminate. Anybody with a computer can create a website and post opinions and interpretations without professional oversight. In fact, many essays that you find as the result of an Internet search will have been written by young students with no more knowledge or expertise than you have. Consider the credentials of authors whose material you find on the Internet, and be especially cautious about what information you accept as fact.

Summary

Supplemental research is an important part of the analysis process, one that can contribute to dynamic, unified, and creative productions. Ideas that perhaps would not have occurred to you, or answers to questions that had puzzled you, can result from mining the thoughts of playwrights, theatre artists, and scholars. Although it may be tempting to use such research to get a head start on your analysis, we advise strongly that you first complete your independent play analysis. Use further research to supplement your own interpretation and insights. This will be a valuable last step prior to synthesizing all aspects of your analysis.

NOTES

[1] Tennessee Williams, *Memoirs* (Doubleday, 1975).
[2] Steven Berkoff, *I Am Hamlet* (Grove Press, 1990).
[3] Anthony Sher, *The Year of the King: An Actor's Diary and Sketchbook* (Limelight Editions, 1992).
[4] Richard F. Leavitt (ed.), *The World of Tennessee Williams* (Putnam, 1978).
[5] William Redfield, *Letters from an Actor* (Viking, 1967).
[6] Athol Fugard, *Notebooks, 1960–1977* (Theatre Communications Group, 1984).
[7] David Savran, *In Their Own Words: Contemporary American Playwrights* (Theatre Communications Group, 1988), p. 297–98.
[8] Paul Gottschalk, *The Meanings of Hamlet: Modes of Literary Interpretation since Bradley* (University of New Mexico Press, 1972).
[9] Mary L. Bogumil, *Understanding August Wilson* (University of South Carolina Press, 1999).
[10] Judith Milhous and Robert Hume, *Producible Interpretation: Eight English Plays, 1675–1707* (Southern Illinois University Press, 1985).
[11] Peter D. Arnott, *Public and Performance in the Greek Theatre* (Routledge, 1989).

LEVEL FIVE

Bringing It Together

8

Synthesis

In Chapter 1 we discussed our purpose for studying play analysis: We seek to be ideal contributors to the collaborative process of realizing the written play on the stage before an audience. In other words, our purpose in play analysis (the process of breaking down a play into its constituent parts and analyzing the parts) is to understand fully how the parts can contribute to the play as a whole. Toward this goal of understanding the play as a whole, including understanding its production and performance implications, we have studied elements such as given circumstances, the use of direct address to the audience, degrees of realism and nonrealism, character, and language.

We reiterated that conflict is the essence of drama, and we identified a process for understanding a play's conflict. The conflict-resolution structure is the skeleton around which the parts can be synthesized. Each part we've analyzed and interpreted must fit with our understanding of the play's conflict and its resolution. The result is **synthesis**: the seamless integration of the play's parts.

Conflict vs. Theme

When studying a work of art, we may be asked "What's it about?" And we are expected to identify the work's **theme,** or the unifying or dominant ideas explored in it. For example, asked what Sophocles's *Antigone* is about, some might say it's about the individual versus the state. After all, Antigone is the title character, and she is the one whose bravery in the face of overwhelming power appeals to many of us. Antigone may be the most appealing character; certainly she's the most romantic character. But it is Creon (whom we may not like very much) who drives the play's conflict by placing his power and the state's welfare above everything.

When we use themes and subject matter to describe what a play is about, we may fail to address the central element that makes the play dramatic: its conflict. Assigning theme or subject matter the highest place in play analysis is reductive: It forces us to give the focus of our concentration to one theme over another, thus robbing the play of its richness and complexity. Indeed, *Antigone* has multiple themes.

Among them are the struggle for primacy between the individual and the state, the importance of religious traditions as guidelines for human behavior, the value of family over the state, and the danger of arrogantly assuming the rightness of one's point of view. We could list even more themes that the play introduces. If we focus on theme over conflict, one subject must become more important than another.

Conflict analysis produces a different understanding. By centering play analysis on conflict, we root ourselves in the essence of drama—the struggle between opposing forces—while still allowing for all themes to be explored. By maintaining the primacy of conflict over theme, we avoid analysis based in a subject that happens to inspire us or appeal to us but that is not borne out by the actual development of the play itself.

Although Antigone may be the character with whom many of us identify and sympathize, she is not the person who drives the conflict. That is, she is not the protagonist. Yes, Antigone introduces the conflict between Creon and herself by inviting Ismene to join in burying their brother, and when she violates Creon's orders by burying Polynices she presents him with a situation he chooses to confront. But, from that point forward, Creon drives the conflict.

Even before learning that Antigone violated his edict that nobody bury Polynices, Creon demands the Chorus's support: He tells them that as their leader he must be powerful:

"This I believe: / The state keeps us afloat." He expects everyone's support:

Chorus: Then what are you asking me to do?
Creon: Not to side with anyone who disobeys me.

From this moment on, Creon puts the need for obedience to him and to the state above everything; he demands that Antigone, his son, the guards, and even the prophet Teiresias obey him. When Teiresias warns Creon that he is defying the gods ("You will surrender corpse for corpses, one / Begotten of your loins"), rather than heeding the prophet, Creon determines that he, the state's leader, must prevail. In turn, Creon's acts result in the deaths of Antigone, Haemon, and Eurydice. And it is he who comes to know (comes to *see*) what the blind prophet had told him: His actions have destroyed everything he valued; defeated and demoralized by this realization, he says of himself:

> Creon: Come, take this hot-headed fool away,
> A fool who killed you, my son, in my blindness,
> And you too [his wife, Eurydice], who are lying here; poor fool [himself].
> I do not know
> Which way I am to take, where to lean,
> My hands can do nothing right;
> I am crushed beneath my fate.
> [Exit.]

Perhaps one of the most persuasive reasons to discount Antigone as the protagonist is that she exits to her death while fully one-third of the play remains. In fact, Antigone makes her final exit before Creon learns of Haemon's death, before Creon confronts Teiresias, before Eurydice's suicide, and before Creon realizes that by putting his rule and the state's power above everything, he has destroyed all that he loved. These events that transpire after Antigone's death aren't simply denouement; the boxing match is still going on, and Creon is still throwing punches.

For many of us, Antigone's struggle, that of the lonely individual against the powerful ruler, is appealing; however, Antigone doesn't drive the play from its introductory incident to its climax. Our analysis has shown that Creon rather than Antigone is the play's protagonist; thus, we have avoided the danger of building our understanding of the play around our personal sympathies or preferences. We are ready to identify, analyze, interpret, and integrate the play's many elements, including its themes, into a synthesized understanding grounded in its conflict.

A conflict analysis in which Creon is the protagonist does not preclude exploring the struggle of the individual against the power of the state. Indeed, for a production of *Antigone* to be emotionally fulfilling we must empathize with Antigone. We can admire her will, her determination, her loyalty to family, and her religious feeling. Likewise, we can empathize with Haemon, who sides with his betrothed, Antigone, against his father and the power of the state. We can applaud the blind prophet, Teiresias, who has a spiritual awareness that supersedes Creon's political power. We can celebrate all these emotional identifications. But by building our overall analysis around our understanding of the conflict, we force ourselves to return to the play's through line: Creon's putting his will, his view of right and wrong, above the will of the gods. As a result, he suffers powerfully; he loses all who were dear to him. Out of the suffering comes his self-awareness. He is a tragic protagonist who has committed an act that results in profound suffering, suffering that extends out, like ripples from a stone thrown in the water, from the personal, to the family, and to the state. When Creon realizes what he has done wrong, he arrives at self-awareness. As a result of his new understanding he gains the wisdom and power to restore equilibrium.

Let's use Molière's *Tartuffe* as another example of relating themes and other elements of analysis to a play's conflict.

Tartuffe explores, among several topics, the theme of religious hypocrisy. Tartuffe presents himself as a devoutly religious person, but he doesn't behave the way we expect a religious person to behave: He attempts to seduce Elmire, he tricks Orgon out of his property, and he betrays Orgon to the King.

The destructive power of lust is another theme in *Tartuffe*. Tartuffe, despite his protests of religiosity, lusts after Elmire, so much so that he risks losing Orgon's friendship and protection.

Another major theme involves individuals putting their personal needs above the welfare of friends and family. Tartuffe is so overcommitted to serving his own needs and desires that he betrays his benefactor. Orgon is committed to bringing his entire household under his dominion. He is so committed to Tartuffe and the religiosity that Tartuffe represents that he refuses to believe his wife and his son when they tell him Tartuffe attempted to seduce her. Despite having betrothed Mariane to Valère, Orgon announces she must marry Tartuffe. Orgon's commitment to Tartuffe's religiosity is so great he is prepared to throw everything over:

> Orgon: Yes, thanks to him I'm a changed man indeed.
> Under his tutelage my soul's been freed
> From earthly loves, and every human tie:
> My mother, children, brother, and wife could die,
> And I'd not feel a moment's pain.   (Act I, Scene 5)

Another theme, the importance of balance and reasonableness, is explored through several of Cléante's speeches, for example this speech to Orgon:

> Cléante: Being blind, you'd have all others blind as well;
> The clear-eyed man you call an infidel,
> And he who sees through humbug and pretense
> Is charged, by you, with want of reverence.
> Spare me your warnings, Brother; I have no fear
> Of speaking out, for you and Heaven to hear,
> Against affected zeal and pious knavery.   (Act I, Scene 5)

After Tartuffe's first attempt at seduction, and Damis's hotheaded response, Elmire advocates reasonableness:

> Elmire: Ah no, Damis! I'll be content if he
> Will study to deserve my leniency.
> I've promised silence—don't make me break my word;
> To make a scandal would be too absurd.

> Good wives laugh off such trifles, and forget them;
> Why should they tell their husbands and upset them?   (Act III, Scene 4)

In a sense, the play centers on the idea that we must avoid mechanical overcommitment to any idea or program. We must be balanced, measured, and mindful in our responses to everything.

Must we choose one defining theme from among these possibilities? No. To do so would reduce a play that explores multiple ideas to a single theme. However, if we base our analysis in the play's conflict-resolution structure, we can identify and celebrate them all. Our task, our challenge, is to determine how each theme relates to and grows out of our conflict analysis.

Relating Other Elements to Conflict

In the Introduction, we said that play analysts apply the supreme test of their understanding of the play by creating a narrative statement that synthesizes their analysis. The act of synthesizing their analysis into a written statement tests their ability to bring to bear all of the questions they've asked about the text.

We seek productions that are coherent and synthesized works of theatre art. Ideally every aspect of the play relates in a clear and supportive way to the conflict. Therefore, it is critical that we examine each element of our analysis. To do so we must ask, How does each element contribute to a unified view of the play that is driven by our understanding of the conflict?

Let's propose a conflict analysis that identifies Orgon as the protagonist. After all, he is the character who drives the conflict. In checking the conflict-resolution process, we look first for the climax: Orgon has driven the conflict by insisting on absolute obedience to his will. He has sought almost god-like power over everyone and everything. After the Officer announces that the King has invalidated the deed awarding Orgon's property to Tartuffe, and after the Officer announces that the King, because of Orgon's "loyal deeds in the late civil war," is pardoning Orgon, after all this Orgon still tries to control everything. He turns on Tartuffe and says, "Well, traitor, now you see . . . " Orgon has heard that the King will see to Tartuffe's punishment, but he, Orgon, still intends to control (even beyond the King's control). But Cléante interrupts and tells Orgon that he should stop trying to control everything:

> Cléante: Ah, Brother, please,
> Let's not descend to such indignities.
> Leave the poor wretch to his unhappy fate,
> And don't say anything to aggravate

> His present woes; but rather hope that he
> Will soon embrace an honest piety,
> And mend his ways, and by a true repentance
> Move our just King to moderate his sentence.
> Meanwhile, go kneel before your sovereign's throne
> And thank him for the mercies he has shown. (Act V, Scene 6)

Now either Orgon must accept that Cléante is right and that the King is in control or he must continue his effort to control, in a sense attempting to extend his control beyond the King's. But Orgon finally stops:

> *Orgon:* Well said: let's go at once and, gladly kneeling,
> Express the gratitude which all are feeling.
> Then, when that first great duty has been done,
> We'll turn with pleasure to a second one,
> And give Valère, whose love has proven so true,
> The wedded happiness which is his due. (Act V, Scene 6)

Throughout the play Orgon struggled mechanically, mindlessly to maintain control over everyone in his circle; in the play's final speech he gives up control. In a sense he accepts simultaneously both the powers of God and King, for after all, the King in those times ruled by divine right. Orgon's final speech is the play's climax; He's finally given up the struggle to control everything and everybody.

What is the major dramatic question that is answered in that moment of climax? We propose, Will Orgon return to his humanity and quit trying to impose his rule on everyone?

Is there a denouement? Does the text provide lines that tie up the raveled threads? No, but even though there is no dialogue or stage direction to employ as authority, one can easily imagine, after the final line, Mariane and Damis embracing (for Damis is now free to marry, too), Elmire embracing her husband (the marriage and family are restored to their proper relationship), Cléante and Dorine enthusiastically shaking hands (two of the play's voices of reason and moderation), and Madame Pernelle standing alone, realizing that she has stubbornly held out for the voice of mechanical and mindless adulation of Tartuffe and is now isolated. This describes the way we could create a moment of denouement that is unwritten but that is true to the conflict and to the central characters' relationships.

What is the play's introductory incident, the moment when the subject of the conflict is introduced? Although Orgon is not onstage during the first scene, the subject of his imposing Tartuffe and stiff religiosity on the family is introduced:

Damis:	Good God! Do you expect me to submit To the tyranny of that carping hypocrite? Must we forgo all joys and satisfactions Because that bigot censures all our actions?
Dorine:	To hear him talk—and he talks all the time— There's nothing one can do that's not a crime. He rails at everything, your dear Tartuffe.
Madame Pernelle:	Whatever he reproves deserves reproof. He's out to save your souls, and all of you Must love him, *as my son would have you do*. (Act I, Scene 1) [Italics added.]

Madame Pernelle introduces here the subject of Orgon, her son, demanding that the household ("all of you") must love Tartuffe as Orgon would have them do. Orgon's demand for obedience is introduced here.

What is the moment of engagement? At what moment in the play does Orgon demand their obedience? We can identify two choices: One is the moment when Orgon tells Mariane that she must marry Tartuffe:

Orgon:	Yes, Tartuffe shall be Allied by marriage to this family, And he's to be your husband, is that clear? It's a father's privilege ... (Act II, Scene I)

The other moment is broader and extends to Orgon's putting Tartuffe and religiosity above everything. Arguing with Cléante, who has called Orgon a "goose" for being so blindly committed to Tartuffe, he says,

Orgon:	He is a man who ... a man who ... an excellent man. To keep his precepts is to be reborn, And view this dunghill of a world with scorn. Yes, thanks to him I'm a changed man indeed. Under his tutelage my soul's been freed From earthly loves, and every human tie: My mother, children, brother, and wife could die, And I'd not feel a single moment's pain. (Act I, Scene 5)

The speech in which Orgon demands that Mariane marry Tartuffe is the play's first moment when he performs an act that demands obedience to his will. One could argue that this is the play's moment of engagement. However, the speech in which Orgon tells Cléante that he's been freed from "earthly love," that he's a "changed man," and that he's devoted to Tartuffe's religious precepts is the moment when we see that Orgon's commitment is utter and complete. It is a shocking commitment. He is committed to achieving his will, under the influence of Tartuffe's extreme religiosity, come what may. This moment demonstrates a commitment that lasts throughout the play.

Can the conflict analysis we've presented contain and support the themes we identified earlier? Yes. Nothing in the conflict analysis precludes exploring religious hypocrisy, the dangers of lust, overcommitment to one's own needs, or the importance of balance and reasonableness. These themes can be explored and celebrated along the way to finding out if Orgon will come to his senses and stop imposing his will on everyone in the household.

Given Circumstances

In studying the given circumstances, we must ask, How do they relate to and support the conflict? For example, there's Orgon's belief that it's right for him to marry Mariane, against her will, to Tartuffe. In the upper-middle-class French culture of Molière's time, a father's permission was necessary for his daughter's marriage. Therefore, as long as Orgon wants his daughter to marry Tartuffe, he has the power to keep her from marrying Valère. This is an important given circumstance that supports the conflict.

Presentationalism and Representationalism

In studying the play's theatrical contract, we consider its use of presentationalism. We must notice which characters are given the privilege of speaking directly to the audience, and we must determine how the moments of presentationalism fit into the conflict-resolution structure. For example, the maid, Dorine, has asides that comment on Orgon's blindness in breaking his daughter's engagement and offering her in marriage to Tartuffe:

> Dorine: Well, I'll be quiet. But I'll be thinking hard.
> Orgon: Think all you like, but you had better guard
> That saucy tongue of yours, or I'll . . .
> [Turning back to Marianne.]
> Now, Child,
> I've weighed this matter fully.
> Dorine: [Aside.]
> It drives me wild
> That I can't speak.
> [Orgon turns his head, and she is silent.]
> Orgon: Tartuffe is no young dandy,
> But, still, his person . . .
> Dorine: [Aside.]
> Is as sweet as candy.   (Act II, Scene 2)

We must ask what effect Dorine's asides produce, and how they relate to the conflict. Perhaps she has the privilege of direct address because it helps heighten the play's comic effect. This is a practical consideration that has great appeal. However, we must also justify it dramatically. Both Dorine and Cléante, two voices of reason, have the privilege of direct address. Perhaps their clear-sightedness, expressed directly to the audience, serves to highlight Orgon's blindness in regard to Tartuffe.

Realism and Nonrealism

Molière's comedies were written at a time when the Italian *commedia dell'arte* companies were popular in Europe, and his theatre company shared a Parisian theatre with a *commedia dell'arte* company. His plays used stereotyped characters that were borrowed from, or at least influenced by, the Italian popular comedy. How might this fact connect to the conflict? Traditionally comedies have dealt with characters who overcommit to one point of view or course of action, just as Orgon does. The stereotyped characters (bigger than life and clearly nonrealistic) allow Molière to emphasize this overcommitment to comic effect, even while addressing a serious issue.

The play's abrupt, happy ending seems artificially contrived, consistent with a nonrealistic theatrical contract. The arrival of the King's Officer seems to be like a *deus ex machina* (literally, a god machine, an ancient Greek theatre term referring to the machine used to fly in gods who resolved the characters' problems, usually at the last moment). Orgon's legal problems are resolved happily by the King's Officer, who announces at the last moment that the King, in his wisdom, has seen through Tartuffe's machinations and restored Orgon's property and good name. In many ways, this almost arbitrary ending emphasizes the underlying seriousness of Orgon's comic overcommitment, for without the miraculous intervention of the King's Officer, Orgon and his family were certainly doomed. Again, the conflict is supported through a structural element.

We have reviewed several elements of Molière's *Tartuffe* and found that they are congruent with an analysis that proposes Orgon to be the play's protagonist. Having tested our analysis of these elements, we can synthesize them into a production of *Tartuffe*.

Questions about Synthesis in *The Glass Menagerie*

Synthesizing all elements of *The Glass Menagerie* demands that we determine a conflict analysis and then examine every element of our work in light of the conflict analysis. In Chapter 2 we offered a conflict analysis, which you can use in studying the relationship of the analysis to each element you have analyzed. For example, what given circumstances are most important to this conflict analysis? How do our earlier decisions about the play's contracts relate to the conflict? How is our perception of each character affected by the conflict? Consider the following, more specific questions: How does Tom's job at the factory interact with Amanda's poverty and her concern for Laura's future? One given circumstance is Laura's inability to complete business school. How does that relate to the conflict? Jim brings Laura to life and gives her a hope she's apparently never experienced. How does his treatment of Laura relate to Amanda's struggle to ensure Laura's future?

Are there themes that emerge as being critically important to our conflict analysis? If Amanda is the protagonist, what themes emerge as most important? Freedom versus responsibility? The fierce protectiveness of mothers? The compromises we make in achieving our goals? Do Williams's projections (proposed in stage directions) suggest important themes? For example, "Laura, haven't you ever liked some boy?" Or "The crust of humility"? Williams is famous for his concern for his damaged characters, those who are in some way less capable than others of coping with a brutal outside world. Does our conflict analysis allow us to encompass such an idea if we find that it is present in the play?

The play's themes are too many for us to itemize all of them here, but if we are to synthesize our analysis, we must test how each relates to our conflict analysis. That is, does our conflict analysis allow us to support, even celebrate, the play's themes?

Synthesis demands that we use the conflict analysis interactively as an analytical tool with other elements of our analysis. Once we've identified the conflict, we can return, for example, to our study of the play's given circumstances. As a result of determining the conflict, some circumstances will emerge as being more important than others. In the same way, our observations about a character need to be related to the conflict. For example, Laura's limp is something we think of as being important about her. Undoubtedly it is important at a metaphorical level. But it may be more important to the conflict that she has profound difficulty in dealing with other people, in coping with the world outside the home. Laura's having vomited on the floor at the business school may be as important as her limp.

We use Laura's limp and her response to business school only as examples. Once we determine the conflict, it becomes important that we return to the text, attempting to sift through each element, testing its relationship to the conflict. A touchstone is, by definition, a test for the qualities of a thing. Conflict analysis is our analytical touchstone. We test the qualities of each element of analysis by relating the element to our analysis.

Questions about Synthesis in Any Play

1. How does each element of your analysis contribute to a unified view of the play that is driven by the play's conflict?
2. How have you integrated the play's themes into your analysis?
3. How have you integrated supplemental research into your analysis?

Testing and Enriching Our Analysis through Outside Resources

Consulting outside resources may lead to the discovery of "authorities" who see the play in ways that don't fit our analysis. For example, in the process of writing this book we found analyses of *The Glass Menagerie* that were based in the interpretation of theme rather than conflict analysis. One critic asserted that the play is about Laura and her inability to survive in a violent real world. This kind of assertion requires that we test, compare, and contrast the authority's analysis against our own. We may also find ideas that clarify and illuminate parts of the play that had previously remained hazy despite our analysis. These ideas can be incorporated into our understanding of the play.

Conclusion

We have provided a systematic process for identifying and interpreting important elements of a play, and we have provided terms you can use to communicate with others. By emphasizing the centrality of conflict analysis we provided a touchstone against which you can test the value of each element you've analyzed. By relating each element to the conflict analysis, you can ask central questions about the element and how it functions in the play: How important is this element to my understanding of the play's essence (its conflict)? How can this element be presented to the audience in a way that it supports the conflict? Or is this element only tangentially related to the conflict and therefore an element that I will choose to recognize but not celebrate?

By using systematic play analysis based on conflict analysis, you have the potential to celebrate every element you've identified and analyzed and to communicate this understanding to your audience. That is what we all seek in our struggle to be artists of the theatre.

Appendix 1
Analyzing Shakespeare's *Hamlet*

In this appendix we apply the analysis process to *The Tragedy of Hamlet*, as we did for *The Glass Menagerie* in the main text. Why another play? Why Shakespeare? And why *Hamlet*? We believe studying another play intensively will reinforce your understanding of the analysis system. We chose Shakespeare because we've found that students may need help with his plays. We chose *Hamlet* because it is a great play, one that is frequently cited, anthologized, and produced, and one that is representative of problems inherent in analyzing Shakespeare's plays.

In this book we introduced you to a sequence of topics such as the first reading and given circumstances, devoting a chapter to each and ending each chapter by posing questions to be asked about *The Glass Menagerie*. We modify that process in this appendix. For each major step in the analysis, we introduce information specific to Shakespeare and to *Hamlet* and then pose questions to ask about *Hamlet*.

The Text of *Hamlet*

Whole books have been written about the three versions of *Hamlet* that were printed between 1603 and 1623. For our purposes it is enough to say that a printing called the First Quarto appeared in 1603; this was a garbled, probably pirated, script. Then in 1604 there was a more reliable version, the Second Quarto, which seems to have been authorized by the theatre company with which Shakespeare worked. Then in 1623, seven years after Shakespeare's death, a collection of his plays, including *Hamlet*, was published under the supervision of two of the late playwright's fellow actors. That collection has come to be called the First Folio. (The terms *folio* and *quarto* have to do merely with how many times a book's paper was folded for printing. Folio pages were folded once and were about fifteen inches high; quartos were folded twice and thus were smaller. Folio pages had two columns of print per page, and quartos one column.)

Most contemporary versions of *Hamlet* are the product of scholar-editors who use both the Second Quarto and the First Folio as their sources. When you read the play today, you will probably encounter it in modern print (rather than with S's that look like F's), with modern spelling, and with brackets indicating information such as stage directions that the editor has introduced.

The First Reading

In Chapter 1 we offered recommendations for your first reading of a play: Read it in one sitting, make notes in the margins, note unfamiliar references and words, begin to distinguish between stage directions and dialogue as sources of information, learn to visualize the stage directions, learn to gather information from dialogue, and look for the play's dominant mood. Each technique is relevant to reading *Hamlet*.

Hamlet is a long play. Because it's a play that uncut runs over four hours, few of us have seen a production in which the entire text is spoken. Because of *Hamlet*'s length, it may be difficult to find time to read it in one sitting. Nevertheless, it's worthwhile. You'll gain a sense of its rhythms, and we believe you'll follow the conflict-resolution structure in a much better way than if you read it in multiple sittings.

Many believe *Hamlet* to be among Shakespeare's greatest tragedies. Few plays explore a tragic hero's experience with such depth and perception. The play sweeps from scene to scene in a rhythm that was almost certainly unbroken by intermission in its original performance. Intermission or not, it is critically important to experience the play in one sitting, gaining a sense of its rhythms and its conflict.

Most contemporary editions of *Hamlet* provide footnotes explaining the meaning of obscure words. The language is often archaic, and we need the notes. So let's ignore our usual advice to make notes on word meanings. In fact, when we read Shakespeare, we usually trust editors' notes the first time through. In the first reading of *Hamlet* save your note taking for questions other than word meanings. Later, when you are familiar with the play, you can go to the *Oxford English Dictionary* to address nuances of meaning.

In Shakespeare's time it was uncommon for plays to be printed. Plays were handwritten and seldom copied in full. Actors' parts were handwritten as "sides"; with only the character's cues and speeches written out. (Remember that there were no copying machines, no computer printouts.) It was in a theatre company's interest to limit the circulation of a play.

Analyzing Shakespeare's *Hamlet*

When a play was printed, few, if any, editorial additions were made. The reader saw a printed version of the acting company's handwritten version. Stage directions were few. In both the Second Quarto and the First Folio, *Hamlet*'s stage directions mainly indicate entrances and exits and a few sound effects. There are a few, but very few, directions for specific character actions such as "Enter Hamlet reading on a Booke" or "In scuffling they change Rapiers."

We said earlier that most modern editors of Shakespeare insert in brackets what we might call suggested stage directions. The same bracketing technique is used in texts of Greek and Roman plays and in many plays written before the nineteenth century. Keep in mind that the bracketed stage directions are the work of editors, who have proposed directions for the characters. Some are the editors' inventions, and some are the product of editors studying promptbooks of historical productions.

Even with the bracketed stage directions provided, we still must search the dialogue for much of the information we are accustomed to finding in modern plays' stage directions. Therefore, Shakespeare's dialogue demands more careful reading than we are accustomed to employing. The information is in the dialogue as implied stage directions.

To illustrate how information is embedded in dialogue, demanding discovery and interpretation, let's examine the opening scene from the First Folio (1623) printing of *Hamlet*. We've inserted brackets that indicate our discoveries.

THE TRAGEDIE OF *HAMLET*, Prince of Denmarke.

Actus Primus. Scaena Prima.

Enter Barnardo and Francisco two Centinels.

Barnardo: Who's there?
[*The audience learns from the first speech and from succeeding lines that it's dark night. Implied in the dialogue is the idea that neither Barnardo nor Francisco can see the other. Because Shakespeare's plays were mostly presented out of doors, in the afternoon, dialogue had to carry information about location, time of day, and weather.*]

Francisco: Nay answer me: Stand & unfold your selfe.

Bar: Long live the King.
[*Francisco recognizes Barnardo's voice. We learn there is a king; there will be more information about that later.*]

Fran: Barnardo?

Bar: He.

Appendix 1

Fran: You come most carefully upon your hour.
[We've learned Francisco was expecting Barnardo, or at least he was expecting someone to come. We learn later, from the dialogue, that they are guards, "Centinals," and that Barnardo is here to relieve Francisco.]

Bar: 'Tis now strook twelve, get thee to bed Francisco.
[We learned earlier it's dark. Now we know it's midnight.]

Fran: For this relief much thanks: Tis bitter cold, and I am sicke at heart.
[Some relief is taking place. It's cold. And Francisco is apparently upset.]

Bar: Have you had quiet Guard?
[Here's when we learn they are standing guard.]

Fran: Not a Mouse stirring.

Bar: Well, goodnight. If you do meet Horatio and Marcellus, the Rivals of my Watch, bid them make haste.
[Rivals is an example of a word that's changed meaning over the last four hundred years. Here, rivals of the watch means not that they are competitors but that they are partners. They are going to be standing watch with Barnardo.]

Enter Horatio and Marcellus.

[It's dark, so Barnardo and Francisco can't see Horatio and Marcellus, or at least that's the theatrical contract. We can imagine that Horatio and Marcellus are looking about as if it were so dark they cannot see Francisco and Barnardo, even though they are onstage with them, a few feet away.]

Fran: I think I hear them. Stand: who's there?

Horatio: Friends to this ground.

Marcellus: And Leige-men to the Dane.
[From this information and the earlier reference to the king, we learn by deduction that they are in service to the King of Denmark.]

Fran: Give you good night.
[The implied stage direction is that Francisco crosses the stage to the point that he, Horatio, and Marcellus can see each other, but Marcellus can't yet see Barnardo.]

Mar: O farewell honest Soldier, who hath reliev'd you?
[We've learned they're soldiers.]

Fran: Barnardo ha's my place: give you goodnight.

Exit Fran.

Mar:	Holla Barnardo.
	[Marcellus still can't see Barnardo. He's saying, Hey, is that you Barnardo?]
Bar:	Say, what is Horatio there?
	[Barnardo thinks it was Horatio speaking.]
Hor:	A piece of him.
Bar:	Welcome, Horatio, welcome good Marcellus.
	[Sometime between "is Horatio there?" and "Welcome, Horatio," Barnardo has recognized them.]

Look back now, and consider that much of what might, in some play scripts, be printed as stage directions has been implied in this scene's dialogue. You may want to look at various editions of the play to see which editors provide the greatest help in finding stage directions in the dialogue. We've learned that in analyzing Shakespeare we must finally do the hard work ourselves, not trusting any editor to give us all the information embedded in the dialogue. Plus, the editors tend to be literary scholars, not persons who are used to having to transform written information into action on the stage.

Given Circumstances

Special Problems in *Hamlet*'s "When" and "Where"

Shakespeare and his contemporaries often set their plays in the past, but they approached history with relative freedom from the need to present only documented facts. We can't be sure with any Shakespearean play what history the audience knew. It is possible, but unlikely, that the audience knew of a ninth-century Danish prince named Amleth, and the audience may have known of an earlier London play about Hamlet. But there is little reason to believe Shakespeare's audience was concerned with what we think of as historical accuracy.

We know from the title that Hamlet is a "Prince of Denmark." As you read the play, does it seem important where *Hamlet* is set? Does it seem important when it is set? Does the play create a sense of happening long before Shakespeare's time? Recently? Do these questions of when and where seem important?

The Shakespearean scholar Northrop Frye commented on the play's anachronistic mix of historical and present time: "In *Hamlet* . . . we seem most of the time to be in Denmark of the Dark Ages, but Hamlet is a student at Wittenberg, a university founded around 1500, and Laertes appears to be going off to a kind of Renaissance Paris."[1]

Hamlet, like many of Shakespeare's plays, is anachronistic, mixing a semihistorical Denmark with references to recent events in London of the 1600s. For example, when Hamlet learns from Rosencrantz that touring players have arrived, there is talk of adult professional actors being out of favor. This is almost certainly a reference to the London of Shakespeare's day, in which boy actors, the Children of the Chapel, were popular.

We might say that no matter where or when Shakespeare's plays were set, the characters seem a lot like Englishmen of Shakespeare's time. Do you find examples of characters seeming English? Or do they seem Danish? What seems Danish about them? What seems English? Is it important? Norway borders on Denmark. Is that important in the play? If so, how is it important?

Given Circumstances: Stated and Implied

We demonstrated earlier that *Hamlet*'s first scene demands that we study dialogue as a major source of stage directions. The First Folio of *Hamlet* doesn't even provide a list of characters.

Typical of questions about the given circumstances are these from the opening scene:

1. How do we learn that the Ghost is, or may be, that of the dead king?
2. When Horatio says the Ghost "usurp'st this time of night" he's saying the Ghost doesn't belong here. Does that imply that the Ghost doesn't belong here because dead people shouldn't walk? Because it's night? Does he imply that the Ghost is usurping by impersonating the dead King?
3. Is it stated or implied that the guards believe in ghosts?
4. In a later scene the Ghost tells Hamlet that he has come from "purgatory." Purgatory is a Christian concept, a place where the soul goes before progressing to heaven or hell. Are there other stated or implied Christian references in the opening scene?

Events and Relationships that *Precede* the Play

1. The elder Hamlet's murder precedes the play. How does Hamlet learn his father was murdered? Does Hamlet believe the Ghost? Or does Hamlet believe he must confirm somehow that Claudius killed the elder Hamlet?
2. What does Hamlet learn from the Ghost about Claudius's murdering him?
3. When did Claudius and Gertrude marry?
4. What relationship existed between Hamlet and Ophelia before the play? How do we learn of this relationship?

5. What relationship between Denmark and Norway precedes the play? How do we learn of this relationship?

Social Systems that Affect the Characters

Political Systems

Throughout Shakespeare's career, plays were submitted to a censor, a representative of the Crown who examined the plays, attending to issues of politics and religion. The play could be performed only after gaining approval.

Setting the play in an historical Denmark enabled Shakespeare to create political "rules" for *Hamlet* different from England's under Elizabeth. Succession to the throne was a sensitive issue in Elizabeth's England, an issue that had resulted in conflict prior to Elizabeth's coronation and that was looming again because she had no heirs.

1. What does the play assume about how succession to the kingship is achieved? Does it tell us why the elder Hamlet's brother, Claudius, succeeded to the throne rather than Hamlet?
2. What political roles does Polonius seem to play?
3. Shakespeare's plays often reflect a less than positive attitude toward the public and its lack of wisdom. Is that attitude reflected in *Hamlet*? How does this seem important to the conflict?
4. Denmark under Hamlet's father was in conflict with Norway. How does this political conflict between Denmark and Norway factor into the play's conflict?

Economic Systems

Economics seem unimportant to *Hamlet*. Does the play refer at all to an economic system? If so, how?

Religious Systems

As early as its first scene, *Hamlet* introduces Christian references. Issues of purgatory, heaven, hell, and Christian burial are woven into the play's conflict. Because religion is important to the play, it is helpful to be aware of the religious situation in Shakespeare's England.

Sixteenth-century England experienced intense, often violent religious upheaval. King Henry VIII ruled England at the beginning of the century, initially as a Roman Catholic. Later he outlawed Roman Catholic worship and had himself proclaimed head of the Church of England. In the process of establishing the Church of England, he forcibly appropriated Roman Catholic Church property, keeping some for the Crown and distributing some to loyal supporters. Henry's son, King Edward VI, continued appropriating Church property and abolishing vestiges of Roman Catholicism. However, when Edward VI died, his sister, Queen Mary I, succeeded him and undertook to reestablish Catholicism. Her rule employed so much religious violence that she is referred to in English history as Bloody Mary.

When Mary I died, Henry VIII's other daughter, Elizabeth I, succeeded her in 1558 and returned England to Protestant rule. Shakespeare was born in 1564 and wrote under her rule and that of her successor, King James I, another Protestant.

Under both Elizabeth and James religious controversy continued. The Roman Catholic Church's Pope excommunicated Elizabeth, and Roman Catholic Spain attacked England, attempting but failing to restore Catholicism. England chose James, reigning King of Scotland, to succeed Elizabeth in large measure because they could depend on his continuing England's Protestant rule. Throughout Shakespeare's life, Catholic spies were sent from Spain, and there were almost constant threats on Elizabeth's and James's lives.

1. Denmark was a Catholic country during the time when Amleth, the "source" of *Hamlet*, would have lived. England was Protestant when the play was first performed. Is it clear that the play assumes either version of Christianity (Protestant or Catholic)? Does it seem important whether *Hamlet*'s Denmark is Protestant or Catholic?
2. Is the priest who conducts Ophelia's funeral Catholic or Protestant? Does it seem to matter? Is the priest treated sympathetically?
3. How do questions of purgatory, heaven, hell, and the Devil figure in Hamlet?
4. What are we to understand about the Ghost's relationship to purgatory?
5. Hamlet worries that the Ghost may be a creature of the Devil. How does that affect Hamlet's actions? How is it important to the conflict?
6. One of the continuing controversies about the play has to do with Hamlet's so-called indecision, what critics call his failure to kill Claudius as soon as possible. What does the relationship among purgatory, heaven, and hell have to do with Hamlet's initial decision to avenge his father's death? What does it have to do with Hamlet's decision not to kill Claudius when he is at prayer?
7. *Hamlet* contains multiple references to suicide. How is it a religious issue?

Cultural Norms

Class

1. The play takes place at and near the Danish castle, the seat of Danish rule, and the play's social behavior seems to be guided by the court. There seem to be rules of behavior between royalty and non-

royalty. How do these rules affect the way characters behave toward each other?
2. How do the play's commoners behave toward the royalty? How do these differences seem important?

Ethnicity

1. *Hamlet* involves characters of three ethnic groups: Danes, Norwegians, and English Ambassadors who appear in the final scene. In addition, there are the "Players," whose nationality is unidentified. Do these characters behave in ways that mark them as being ethnically different from each other? For example, Fortinbras is Norwegian, as is his Captain. Does either of them speak or behave in ways that identify them as ethnically different from the Danish characters?
2. Dialogue refers to Claudius's court being given to excessive drinking that reflects badly on Denmark's image. Does this factor into the conflict in any substantial way?
3. After the murder of Polonius, Claudius sends Hamlet to England, having arranged with the English King for Hamlet's murder. Is it significant that he sends Hamlet to England?

Marriage and Family

1. Under most rules of royal succession in Shakespeare's time, primogeniture would have prevailed. That is, Prince Hamlet, the late king's son, would inherit the kingship. Does the play account for Claudius rather than Hamlet becoming King?
2. Claudius refers to having killed his brother as a rank offense that has "the primal eldest curse upon't." This seems to be a reference to Cain's murder of Abel. Are there biblical references that apply to marrying a brother's widow?
3. What do Polonius and Laertes seem to believe about Hamlet's interest in marrying Ophelia? What does Ophelia seem to believe? Is there evidence that Hamlet intends (intended) to marry Ophelia?
4. Does the play begin with a happy marriage existing between Claudius and Gertrude? Does the marriage change after Hamlet tells his mother how she should treat Claudius?
5. What other family dynamics are at work in the play?

Language Use

It has been argued that Shakespeare's plays represent the most powerful use of language in all of dramatic literature. His vocabulary is estimated as being two to three times larger than that of today's educated person.

Formal education in Shakespeare's time was not as pervasive as it is today. Few Englishmen attended university. Most had what was called a grammar school education. However, even those with only a grammar school education had studied some classical literature of the Greeks and the Romans. It was a culture that celebrated language. People went to the theatre in Shakespeare's day to "hear" a play. Today we speak of going to "*see*" a play. The difference is reflected in the plays of Shakespeare and his contemporaries.

The importance of language is a given circumstance of all Shakespearean plays, but it is especially important as a given circumstance of *Hamlet*. The play celebrates Hamlet's complexity of thought, thought spoken aloud about an immense range of topics: the meaning of life, death, suicide, and the hereafter. He wonders aloud about his actions and his failure to act. He is a creature of language, devoted to language both as a means of communicating to others and as a tool for understanding himself.

Hamlet's dialogue alternates between poetry and prose. Sometimes it distinguishes between public and private conversations, but at other times it is not immediately clear why characters speak in verse or prose. How does the mixture of poetry and prose in *Hamlet* seem to relate to the given circumstances? Is there a consistent pattern? Are the shifts associated sometimes with Hamlet's changes of mood? Are there moments when it is difficult to determine his purpose in switching from poetry to prose or the reverse?

1. How does Hamlet's use of prose and poetry relate to his pretended madness?
2. It can be said of Shakespeare's characters that they think "on the word, not between the words." This means that they do not hesitate or stumble, trying to find words to express their thoughts; the words are readily available to them. Might we think of this fluency as a given circumstance for all the play's characters?
3. Is there a difference between the two gravediggers in their ability to use language? Is the First Gravedigger as verbal as Hamlet?
4. Does the play use language to distinguish among ethnic groups?
5. Does the play use language to distinguish between royalty and nonroyalty?

Theatrical Contract

Presentational and Representational

Printed plays from Shakespeare's time give no indication of asides or soliloquies. Modern editors sometimes provide stage directions indicating asides, but they are occasionally unreliable in this regard. You will be served best by searching on your own for asides. Editors are equally undependable in regard to identifying soliloquies. We recommend a general rule: Think of characters who are alone onstage as unself-consciously addressing the audience, sharing their points of view with us, trusting that when we understand them and their emotional plights we will support them.

1. Claudius is given the privilege of a major monologue: his speech about his guilt and his difficulty with prayer. What does this monologue contribute to the conflict?
2. Can you identify any progression among Hamlet's monologues? Does his relationship to us change? Does he need us, our support and understanding increasingly or decreasingly as the play progresses?

Realism and Nonrealism

Remember that in thinking of realism and nonrealism we are concerned with the play's treatment or representation of what we might call everyday reality. We are not speaking of plausibility or implausibility. Rather we are concerned with the playwright highlighting elements to focus on them, to emphasize them, and to bring them to our attention.

Shakespeare's plays mix realism and nonrealism. He can be realistic. He develops some of dramatic literature's most fully rounded, most complex characters. His dialogue has an additional element of realism in that his characters sound so profoundly different from each other. They use language that is carefully tuned to situation and relationship. Even though his plots are sometimes careless in their treatment of detail (plausibility), the plays are realistically based in human psychology and in cause-and-effect relationships.

On the other hand Shakespeare's plays contain much that is nonrealistic. His characters speak mostly in iambic pentameter verse that is brilliantly conceived but not realistic. We spoke earlier of anachronism; his plays have little apparent regard for either geographic or historical accuracy. Some of his plays, especially his comedies, use stereotypes created with broad, nonrealistic strokes. Indeed some characters are stereotypes that can be traced back centuries to Roman comedies.

1. In the context of realism and nonrealism, what are the effects of moving between prose and poetry at various times in *Hamlet*?
2. Early in the play's opening scene, Barnardo says the clock just struck twelve. About 170 lines later Horatio sees the sun coming up in the east. We've gone from midnight to dawn in ten minutes. Is Shakespeare being careless here? Is he depending on the audience to accept a nonrealistic contract about the passage of time? Does this scene represent Shakespeare mixing the realistic and nonrealistic?
3. Hamlet may be one of dramatic literature's most complexly drawn characters. He is full of contradictions. He is far from a stereotype. The same may be said, to a lesser degree, of Claudius, Gertrude,

Laertes, and Ophelia. However, the play also has stereotypical, often nonrealistic characters such as Polonius, the Gravedigger, and Osric. What is the effect? How does this mixture affect our experience of the play?

Anachronism and Inconsistency

1. Perhaps more has been written about *Hamlet* than about any other play, and part of this storehouse of literature includes questions about so-called problems in *Hamlet*, problems that emerge from inconsistencies in the plot's details. For example, Hamlet came home for his father's funeral, which is spoken of as having taken place a few weeks ago. His college schoolmates, Horatio, Rosencrantz, and Guildenstern, speak as though they have not seen him for a long time, longer, it seems, than two months ago. Is that an example of careless inconsistency in the playwriting? Or does all this seem to be a conscious dramatic device on Shakespeare's part? If so, what seems to be its purpose?
2. Are there other moments that could be treated as inconsistencies? How should we account for them? Is it likely that Shakespeare intended the play to sweep us along in such a way that we are not concerned with such specific details?

Character, Language, and Thought Process

Hamlet is laden with terrific examples from which we can draw to illustrate the relation among character, language, and thought process. Let's use Claudius's first speech as an example of a thought process that is riddled with dishonesty but representative of our earlier assertion that Shakespeare's characters "think on the word, not between the words." Sometimes they tell outright lies without hesitation. Claudius is not Shakespeare's biggest liar, but he is among them. His approach to lying is representative of Shakespeare's characters who lie: They lie quickly and well. Later they may tell the audience that they were lying and how they feel about the lies.

From the Folio stage directions we know Gertrude, Hamlet, Polonius, Laertes, Ophelia, and "Lords and Attendants" are present at a state occasion. Sometimes it is staged as a banquet, sometimes as a scene in which the King is holding forth at court:

> King: 'Though yet of Hamlet our dear Brother[']s death
> The memory be green: and that it us befitted
> To bear our hearts in grief, and our whole Kingdom

["Bear our hearts in grief" implies to his listeners that Claudius himself grieved. We learn later that he killed his brother and that Claudius's grief was and is a guise, a cover-up. Throughout the speech he uses rhetorical devices, turns of phrase that will impress his audience with his verbal skills.]

To be contracted in one brow of woe:
Yet so far hath Discretion fought with Nature,
That we with wisest sorrow think on him,
Together with remembrance of our selves.

[One meaning of irony is for a person to use words to express a meaning other than the real or opposite meaning. We learn later that Claudius is pretending to sorrow that he doesn't feel. In fact his discretion has fought with his nature: He chooses, discreetly, to put on the appearance of sorrow. He has unnaturally killed his brother. Indeed, he thinks about his brother in remembrance of himself: His kingship was achieved by killing his brother.]

Therefore our sometimes Sister, now our Queen,

[Later he admits to us and to himself that he committed the sin of Cain: murdering his brother. This makes it even more ironic for him to refer to Gertrude as sister and queen.]

Th' imperial joyntress of this warlike State,
Have we, as 'twere, with a defeated joy,
With one Auspicious, and one Dropping eye,

[The mixture of feelings about the marriage and the kingship is complicated: Claudius is pretending that it's all about the paradox of his joy in marriage and his sadness for his brother's death. He knows in his own mind that there's more to the paradox: He's gained his wife and throne only through a primal sin that causes him, in a sense, to be unable to enjoy the things for which he's lied and killed.]

With mirth in Funeral, and with Dirge in Marriage,
In equal Scale weighing Delight and Dole
Taken to Wife; nor have we herein barred
Your better Wisdoms, which have freely gone
With this affair along, for all our Thanks.

[There is irony, too, in that Gertrude and Polonius have gone along with what has happened. Do they know of the murder? No. Have they participated in the hasty funeral, marriage, and crowning of Claudius as the new king? Yes.]

We have chosen only a portion of one speech for examination mainly of one issue: lying and its ironic use. Consider other characters and their situational use of language:

1. *Hamlet* sets up multiple family relationships: son-father, son-stepfather, son-mother, and daughter-father. How does the language of each relationship show who the character is in relation to parent or offspring?
2. The play presents three sons of murdered fathers: Fortinbras, Laertes, and Hamlet. How does language define each son's attitude toward revenging his father's death?
3. Polonius sometimes seems stereotypical and foolish. How does the way he speaks to Laertes differ from the way he talks to Ophelia? How does he speak differently when addressing Claudius and Gertrude?
4. Can the progression of Ophelia's madness be traced in the progression of her language as she deals with others?
5. Study Claudius's language throughout his first scene (Act I, Scene 2). Does his language make him seem to be headed toward political success as king? Does his language make him seem to be a loving husband and father?
6. Above, we traced one aspect of Claudius's thought process: lying and irony. Study the entire scene, concentrating on Claudius's language. What does it demonstrate about the way he thinks, about his process of association? Does he seem to have an agenda? Or does he seem to improvise from moment to moment?
7. Hamlet is one of the most introspective characters in all of dramatic literature. Does the language of his introspection change as the play goes on? How is it situational, growing out of what has just happened in the preceding scene? Does the language of his monologues demonstrate changes in his relationship to the audience?
8. What do you learn about Hamlet from the way he speaks to others? How is he situational in the way he speaks to others?

Conflict Analysis

Is Hamlet the protagonist? If he isn't, who are the alternative protagonists? It could hardly be the Ghost; he doesn't reappear after the scene in Gertrude's bedroom. Could it be Claudius? Possibly, but the play seems to be more concerned with Hamlet's revenging his father's death than it is with Claudius's struggle to hold the throne. Hamlet learns from his father that Claudius murdered him. He swears to revenge his father's murder by killing Claudius.

1. Let's assume the above analysis is correct: Hamlet is the protagonist. What is the moment of climax? Does it come in the moment

when Claudius dies? Are there alternative moments of climax? For example, could it be the moment in which Hamlet dies?
2. If the conflict is resolved in the moment of Claudius's death, what major dramatic question is answered in that moment?
3. If there is an alternative moment of climax, what question is answered in that moment?
4. Hamlet seeks Claudius's death from the scene of his first encounter with the Ghost, but he operates with constraints, things he will or won't do to get his revenge. What are his constraints in regard to Gertrude? What part does religious belief play in Hamlet's constraints?
5. When is the subject of the conflict introduced? Is it introduced in the first scene when the Ghost appears to the guards? Is it introduced in the scene at court when we first see Hamlet and Claudius interact? Is it introduced in the scene between the Ghost and Hamlet?
6. At what moment in the play does Hamlet commit himself to revenging his father's death?
7. Critics have written about Hamlet's indecision, his inability to act. Does he have moments when he fails to act on his commitment? Or can all those moments be accounted for by saying Hamlet is seeking revenge under the right conditions?
8. What happens during the play's denouement? Is it important that all three of the revenge-seeking sons are present onstage at the end of the play?
9. Early in the play, Hamlet makes no protestations that he should have been king. Late in the play he says he should have been king. How does this change relate to Fortinbras?
10. If the moment of Claudius's death is the climax, what function does the subsequent interaction between Laertes and Hamlet serve?
11. Classic tragedies often introduce a world that is in disorder, and they often end with a world restored to order. In what ways is the world disordered in *Hamlet*'s opening scene? (Physical? Political? Social? Religious?) And how does the denouement serve to show that order has been restored?

Supplemental Research

It is possible that more has been written about *Hamlet* than any other play and that more has been written about Shakespeare than any other playwright. Listed here are a few of the books we have found most useful.

General Background

Epstein, Norrie. *The Friendly Shakespeare: A Thoroughly Painless Guide to the Bard.* New York: Penguin, 1994.
This informally written book answers most of the questions you were afraid to ask in class.

Papp, Joseph, and Elizabeth Kirkland. *Shakespeare Alive!* New York: Bantam, 1988.
This book is useful for students who need a general orientation to Shakespeare and his times.

Biography

Schoenbaum, Samuel. *William Shakespeare: A Compact, Documentary Life.* London: Oxford University Press, 1988.
This is the best biography for finding facts—the documented information about Shakespeare—rather than conjecture about him.

Reference

Partridge, Eric (ed.). *Shakespeare's Bawdy.* New York: Routledge, 1991.
This book is where you find out what the "dirty" or "sexy" parts mean.

Simpson, J. A., and E. S. C. Weiner. *The Oxford English Dictionary.* London: Oxford University Press, 1989.
This dictionary records the evolution of meanings of words. It is especially helpful in determining what a word or phrase meant in Shakespeare's time.

Play Texts

Shakespeare, William. *Mr. William Shakespeare's Comedies, Histories, & Tragedies: A Facsimile Edition*, prepared by Helge Kokeritz and Charles Tyler Prouty. New Haven, CT: Yale University Press, 1954.
The title of this book is self-explanatory. It is a photographic reproduction of Yale University's folio edition of Shakespeare's plays. The folio version is especially valuable for Shakespeare's original punctuation, which can be helpful to actors.

Shakespeare, William. *Applause First Folio Editions*, edited by Neil Freeman. New York: Applause Books.
These paperback acting editions present the folio text in modern typeface.

Shakespeare, William. *Arden Shakespeare* [individual plays], edited by Eric Partridge. London: Oxford University Press, 1997.
The Arden Shakespeare series offers excellent notes. The Arden edition of *Hamlet* is almost six hundred pages long, containing brief footnotes regarding word meanings and editorial decisions, as well as

"Longer Notes" that explain a variety of textual issues and answer some questions regarding how the play might be staged.

Synthesis

1. What is the play's conflict? And how does the conflict relate to the play's themes?
2. Will Hamlet revenge his father's death by killing Claudius? Perhaps this is the play's major dramatic question. Are all these elements necessary: Hamlet, father, revenge, killing, and Claudius? Part of the analysis process involves being certain we have included and excluded the necessary pieces in the conflict-resolution structure.
3. Are there important themes this major dramatic question leaves out? Certainly. No single statement or question could specifically include all of *Hamlet*'s themes. There are too many. Among the themes we have identified are heaven and earth; natural versus unnatural; duty of son to father as reflected in three different relationships; truth and lying; a daughter's happiness versus her father's and her brother's fear of sexual disgrace; emotional control versus being "passion's slave"; haste versus delay; sowing, planting, and flowering; sex, lust, and adultery; life after death; purgatory, hell, and the afterlife; both commoners and kings decay after death; poisons and infections; men versus beasts; allegiance, hell, blackness, and damnation; remembering: the importance of remembering, remembering to revenge, and remembering as the source of madness; words versus action; delay versus action; friends, loyalty, and betrayal; Christian death, purgatory, and hell; the Bible, Adam, Cain, and the curse of Cain's killing Abel; and madness feigned by Hamlet and suffered by Ophelia.

The major dramatic question cannot address all these themes. What is important is that we identify the most important themes and explore how they relate to the central conflict.

How to Set *Hamlet*?

For many years theatre practice in the Western world has encouraged producers of Shakespeare to consider the question, When and where should we set his plays? The question is valid. We have seen how *Hamlet* is full of anachronism. To the best of our knowledge, Shakespeare's plays were produced originally on a relatively bare stage and mostly in the clothes of Shakespeare's day. In other words, the dialogue's anachronism apparently extended to the staging. So, as silly as it may sound, *Hamlet* may have been staged with a Ghost who wore medieval armor, alongside a cast wearing Elizabethan doublet and hose (fashionable contemporary clothes).

For centuries after Shakespeare's time his plays were performed on English and American stages with the actors wearing the fashionable clothes of their day. An engraving of an eighteenth-century London production shows Hamlet and Gertrude in contemporary clothes of the day and the Ghost in armor that appears to be medieval.

We might say there is no way we can stage Shakespeare with historical accuracy: Would we do it with most characters in today's clothes but one (perhaps the Ghost) in a suit of medieval armor? No. That seems silly. So what guidance have we for staging his plays?

Our recommendation is to use the conflict as your source of guidance in searching for a period and place suitable for the play. Pose your question as follows: In what historical period and place can we set the play in a way that will communicate its conflict and its major themes clearly to its audience? We cannot answer the question for you. Be assured that major productions have set *Hamlet* as long ago as medieval Denmark and as recently as the present day. The important issue is to make certain the setting supports your analysis: the given circumstances, the contract, the characters and their language, but most especially your analysis of the conflict.

Note

[1] Robert Sandler (ed.), *Northrop Frye on Shakespeare* (New Haven, CT: Yale University Press, 1986), 101.

Appendix 2
Character Maps

A character map is a visual way to represent the connections and relationships between characters in a play. It can be used for quick reference when you are first getting acquainted with a play or later as a way of exploring and discovering patterns within it.

The basic building blocks of a character map are squares (or circles) and arrows. The square represents a character, and the arrow represents a relationship between two squares. For instance, if Character A is Character B's mother, you would represent this as follows:

The direction of the arrow indicates the relationship. The above map would read, Character A is the mother of Character B. We could also charge the direction of the arrow:

This map would read, Character B is the son of Character A.

This technique can be used as a method for visually exploring a variety of relationships: social, emotional, power, and the like. In Chapter 5 we indicated that it is valuable to know the quality of the relationships at the start of the play, and a character map can be used to represent that as well. If Character A hates Character B at the beginning of the play, this could be shown as follows:

Because of the directional nature of the arrows, you can simultaneously show the feelings each character has toward the other. If Character A hates Character B, but Character B loves Character A, you could show it as follows:

The following character map identifies the basic relationships among the characters in *The Glass Menagerie*:

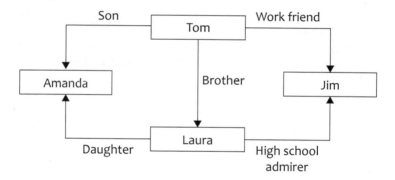

Mapping a play with as many characters as *Romeo and Juliet* can be a challenge, of course. To do so, you will find it necessary to group characters in order to make the map organized and comprehensible, which can help you to recognize patterns. For instance, if you were mapping *Romeo and Juliet*, you might notice the following pattern:

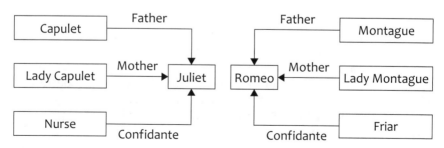

Character Maps

Although such a map might seem fairly obvious, it could lead you to recognize parallels between the Nurse and Friar that you might not have noticed before. It might also lead you to explore whether similar parallels exist between the other characters (Mercutio and Tybalt, for instance). Perhaps you would ask whether the two families are more alike than different (mirror images, perhaps). This metaphor might lead to design choices that would emphasize the two families' similarities. For instance, the costumes of the Montagues might be red with blue accents, and the Capulets' might be blue with red accents. Thus, it is possible that the visual aspect of a character map could reveal aspects of the play's structure that are then played out in its conflict.

Character maps can be useful during all stages of the analysis process as your knowledge of the characters increases and the connections among them become more complex. It is both an organizational and an analytical tool that will help you to recognize connections and remember them later.

Key Terms

Abstraction In nonrealistic productions, the removal from everyday life of some elements of the play. We may think of abstraction existing on a continuum from mere heightening of an element to severe distortion.
Action A character's main intent in a scene. (See also *beat*.)
Aside A device in which a character breaks from dialogue with other characters and speaks directly to the audience.
Backstory The events and relationships that precede the beginning of the play. Some authors also use the term *exposition* to refer to these events and relationships. Backstory is a film term that has come into common use in recent times.
Beat A unit of intent that is smaller, more momentary than an *action*.
Characters The individual persons who appear in the play.
Climax The most important moment in the conflict-resolution structure: the moment when the conflict is resolved. After this moment there is no longer conflict.
Conflict The essence of drama. Conflict grows out of two or more characters having mutually opposed motives.
Conflict-resolution structure The process through which the play introduces and resolves its conflict. It is characterized by progression from introductory incident, to moment of engagement, to climax, to denouement.
Denouement The moments after the climax, in which loose ends of the story are tied up.
Dialogue Usually, speech between two or more characters. *Dialogue* may refer to speech by a single character on stage, speaking to herself or to the audience.
Given circumstances Information regarding the play's background and environment; categories of given circumstances include the events and relationships that precede the play, the play's time and place, the social systems that affect the characters, and the cultural conditions and assumptions under which the characters live.
Internal obstacles Limits that characters apply to themselves in seeking their objectives; obstacles that may preclude some actions.
Introductory incident The moment in the play when the subject of the conflict is introduced. The event must occur in the play, not before the play begins.

Major dramatic question The question that is answered in the moment of climax. This question has been pursued from the introductory incident to the climax.

Moment of engagement The point in the play, after the introductory incident, when the protagonist commits to satisfying her goals.

Mood The feelings evoked by the play. At the extremes, the mood may be one of joy or comedy versus one of sadness or even tragedy.

Nonrealistic contract Theatrical contracts in which one or more elements of production are heightened in a fashion that removes them from resembling the way they appear in everyday life. For example, most of Shakespeare's characters speak in iambic pentameter blank verse that is heightened from everyday speech.

Opposing characters or forces One or more characters having motives that oppose the protagonist's.

Play analysis The process of identifying the constituent parts of a play; interpretation involves clarifying our understanding of the parts we have identified.

Plot The terms *plot* and *story* are often used interchangeably to refer to the series of incidents that make up a play, a film, or a piece of fiction. According to some authors, plot refers to the most important events in a narrative, whereas story refers to the events in sequence, including both most and least important events.

Presentational contract Theatrical contracts in which one or more characters engage occasionally in direct address to the audience. The audience is recognized as being present.

Protagonist The character whose motives and actions drive the play's conflict from its beginning to its resolution.

Realistic contract Theatrical contracts in which most elements of production conform to everyday reality. For example, characters use prose language that resembles everyday speech.

Representational contract Theatrical contracts in which the characters maintain an imaginary fourth wall between the production and the audience. There is no direct address to the audience.

Scene A unit of conflict that has a beginning, a middle, and an end.

Soliloquy A form of dialogue in which a character who is alone on stage addresses the audience directly.

Songs A musical interlude during which a character may or may not sing directly to the audience.

Stage directions Suggestions or instructions, often from the playwright, regarding the play's setting, sound, and lighting effects, and perhaps characters' appearance or behavior.

Synthesis Interpretation and integration of the parts of the play we have analyzed.

Tactics The strategies characters use to get what they want from others.

Theatrical contract An informal understanding created between a production and its audience. The contract has two important aspects: Is the production presentational or representational? And are the elements of production realistic or nonrealistic?

Theatrical conventions Techniques shared by a majority of plays in specific epochs of theatre history. For example, the singing and dancing chorus was a convention of ancient Greek tragedy.

Theme Unifying or dominant ideas explored in a work of art.

Index

Abstraction, in nonrealistic contracts, 58, 61
Accuracy of given circumstances, 38
Acting editions of plays, 13
Action
    characters defined through, 6
    physical, dialogue suggesting, 71–72
Actions and beats, breaking down character motives into, 7, 84–85
Anachronism in Shakespeare, 38, 120
Analysis. *See* Conflict analysis; Play analysis
Antagonist. *See* Opposing force(s)
Antigone (Sophocles)
    characters' responses to given circumstances in, 44, 67
    existing relationships in, 66–67
    presentational theatrical contract in, 57
    social systems affecting characters in, 41
    theme related to conflict in, 98–99
Aristophanes, 43
Aristotle, influence of, 6
Arnott, Peter D., 92
Asides, in presentational contracts, 55, 57
Audience
    identification, through direct address, 56
    theatrical contract with, 53–62

August: Osage County (Letts), 56
Aura, 49
Autobiographical materials, supplemental research using, 88–89

Backstory, as part of given circumstances, 39, 45
Barry, Philip, 42
Beats and actions, breaking down character motives into, 84–85
Berkoff, Steven, 88
Biographical materials, supplemental research using, 88–89
Bogumil, Mary L., 91
Brook, Peter, 91

Cat on a Hot Tin Roof (Williams), 90
Character maps, 127–129
Characters
    being in action, 85
    conflict evoked through, 72–73
    dialogue as source of information about, 17–18
    existing relationships of, 65–67
    general questions regarding, 77
    given circumstances of, 37–51, 67
    intent of, described through actions and beats, 84–85
    language use and given circumstances of, 42–43, 70–71
    motives, breaking down into actions and beats, 84–85

as opposing force, 31
physical actions defined through dialogue, 71–72
points of view of, 68–69
simple vs. complex behavior of, 67–68
social systems affecting, 40–41, 47
stage directions and, 69
tactics used by, 68
Climax
definition of, 28
questions for testing, 32–34
role in conflict analysis/resolution, 29
in *The Glass Menagerie*, 31–32, 80–81
Clothing, cultural norms reflected by, 42
Comedies, essential structures of, 20
Conflict
character revealed through, 72–73
dramatic, structure of, 27–28
as essence of drama, xi
greatest, moment of, 76
presentational theatrical contracts and, 104
process for determining, 28–31
relating elements of a play to, 101–105
in *The Glass Menagerie*, 31–34
theme vs., 97–201
trajectory of, 30, 32
Conflict analysis
through actions and beats, 85
applied to a scene, 79–86
climax and denouement in, 28–29
defining the major dramatic question, 29–30
in *Hamlet*, 122–123
levels of, 3–5
opposing force, role in, 26–27
protagonist function in, 26
realism and, 105
synthesis of play's elements and, 106
in *The Glass Menagerie*, 31–34
Conflict-resolution structure, general questions about, 86

Cultural norms as given circumstances, 41–43
ethnicity, attitudes regarding, 41
marriage, family, and the sexes as, 42
in *The Glass Menagerie*, 48–50

Denouement, 28, 84
Dialogue, gathering information from, 16, 71–72
Direct address, audience identification through, 56–57
Doing
dialogue as, 18
play analysis leading to, 11
Doll's House, A (Ibsen), 56
Dramas, essential structures of, 3, 20
Dramatic conflict. *See* Conflict
Dramatic question, major, 29–30

Economic systems affecting characters, 48
Equus (Shaffer), 56, 59
Ethnicity, 41, 48–49, 75
Existing relationships
characters defined through, 65–66
in *The Glass Menagerie*, 73–74

Family, cultural norms of, 42, 49, 122
Fantastical settings, 43
Farquhar, George, 40
Fichandler, Zelda, 6
First reading techniques
first impressions and, 3, 12
for *Hamlet*, 110–113
noting unfamiliar references and words, 13
reading a play in one sitting, 12
for *The Glass Menagerie*, 20–22
visualizing stage directions, 13–14
Fugard, Athol, 89

Gadamer, Hans-Georg, 28
Gathering information
the first reading, 11
organizing information, 51
See also Given circumstances; Theatrical contract(s)

Index

Given circumstances, 37–51
  accuracy of, 38
  backstory as part of, 39, 45
  characters' responses to, 67
  conflict relating to, 104
  cultural norms as part of, 41–43
  general questions about, 50
  in *Hamlet*, 113–118
  organizing information about, 51
  plays that emphasize, 44
  setting as part of, 39–40, 45
  social systems as part of, 40–41
  stated and implied, 37–38
  in *The Glass Menagerie*, 44–50, 74–75
Glass Menagerie, The (Williams), 5–6
  abstraction in, 61
  actions and beats in, 85
  backstory, 45
  character map for, 128
  characters in, 73–76
  climax of, 31–32, 80–81
  conflict analysis of, 31–34, 80–84
  cultural norms in, 48–50
  denouement in, 84
  ethnicity in, 75
  existing relationships in, 73–74
  first reading of, 20–21
  given circumstances in, 44–50
  introductory incident in, 32, 82–83
  major dramatic question in, 32, 81–82
  moment of engagement in, 33, 83–84
  opposing force(s) in, 82
  protagonist in, 82
  religion affecting characters in, 85
  setting, 45–47
  stage directions in, 61
  synthesis of elements in, 105–106
  theatrical contract in, 60–61
Gottschalk, Paul, 91

Hamlet (Shakespeare)
  backstory of, 39
  family relationships in, 122
  gathering information from dialogue in, 16–17
  moment of engagement in, 27
  nonrealistic theatrical contract in, 60
  presentational theatrical contract in, 57
  scene as a unit of conflict in, 80
  simple vs. complex behaviors in, 68
  thought process in, 120
Hume, Robert, 92

I Am Hamlet (Berkoff), 88
Ibsen, Henrik, 56
Information gathering, 3–4, 37–62
Internal obstacles, 27
Internet, supplemental research conducted on, 92–93
Interpretation, 4
Interviews as source of supplemental research, 89–90
In Their Own Words: Contemporary American Playwrights (Savran), 89
Introductory incident, 27, 30, 32, 82–83

Joe Turner's Come and Gone (Wilson), 13–15
  characters defined through language use in, 69–71
  climax of, 28
  given circumstances in, 44
  representational contract in, 56
  stage directions in, 69
  structure of, 20

Kott, Jan, 91

Language use, 49–50
  characters defined by, 69–71
  given circumstances defined through, 42–43
  relationship with goals and tactics, 76
  situational, in *Hamlet*, 120–122
Leavitt, Richard F., 89
Letts, Tracy, 56
Literary criticism as supplementary research, 91–92
Location. *See* Place, as part of given circumstances
Lysistrata (Aristophanes), 43

Major dramatic question
  defining, 29–30
  questions for testing, 32–34
  in *The Glass Menagerie*, 32, 81–82

Marriage, cultural norms of, 42, 49
Meanings of Hamlet, The: Modes of Literary Interpretation since Bradley (Gottschalk), 91
Memoirs (Williams), 88
Milhous, Judith, 91
Miss Julie (Strindberg), 56
Molière, 17–18, 20, 26, 44, 67, 69, 79. See also *Tartuffe* (Molière)
Moment of engagement, 27, 31, 33, 83–84
Mood, awareness of, 19

Nonrealistic theater contracts, 54, 57
  abstract elements identified in, 59
  plausibility vs. nonrealism in, 59–61
  relation of nonrealism to conflict, 105
Notebooks: 1960–1977 (Fugard), 89
Note taking, and play analysis, 12–13

Objectives, internal obstacles to, 27
Opposing force(s)
  role in conflict analysis, 26–27, 31
  in *The Glass Menagerie*, 82
Outside resources, play analysis tested and enriched through, 107

Parker, Douglass, 43
Philadelphia Story, The (Barry), 42
Place, as part of given circumstances, 40, 46
Plausibility vs. nonrealism, in nonrealistic contracts, 59–61
Play analysis
  of characters, 65–77
  conflict resolution in. See Conflict analysis
  definition of, 2
  first impressions/first reading of a play, 11–22
  given circumstances and, 37–51
  of *Hamlet*, 109–126
  inventive research in, 39
  multiple levels of play reading, 2–5
  note taking and, 12–13
  reading for information to act upon, 11–12
  reasons for, 1–2
  supplemental research for, 87–93
  theatrical contracts and, 53–62
  of translated plays, 43
Plays
  in fantastical settings, 43
  synthesis of the parts of, 97–107
  translated, 43
Playwright's intentions, value in understanding, 55–56
Plot, Aristotle on, 6–7
Points of view of characters, 68–69
Political systems affecting characters, 41, 47
Presentational theatrical contracts, 54–55, 104
Producible Interpretation: Eight English Plays, 1675–1707 (Milhous and Hume), 91
Production elements, realistic and nonrealistic, 58
Protagonist, 6–7, 26, 30–31, 82–84
Public and Performance in the Greek Theatre (Arnott), 92

Race, in *The Glass Menagerie*, 75
Realism, relation to conflict, 105
Realistic theatrical contracts, 54, 57
Religious systems affecting characters, 41, 48, 75
Representational theatrical contracts, 54–55
  relating to conflict, 104–105
Richard II (Shakespeare), 65
Richard III (Shakespeare), setting of, 40
Riders to the Sea (Synge), 40
Rivals, The (Sheridan), 42
Romeo and Juliet (Shakespeare)
  character mapping for, 128–129
  character revealed through conflict in, 73
  characters' movements embedded in dialogue in, 71–72

Savran, David, 89
Scene, conflict analysis applied to, 79–86
Set description, 14–15
  studying dialogue for, 16

Index

Setting(s)
fantastical, 43
given circumstances and, 39–40, 45
for Shakespeare's *Hamlet*, 125–126
Sex, cultural norms of, 42, 49
Shaffer, Peter, 56
Shakespeare Our Contemporary (Kott), 91
Shaw, George Bernard, 69
Sher, Anthony, 88
Sheridan, Richard Brinsley, 42
Situational behaviors, 75–76
Social systems, impact on characters, 40–41, 47–48
Soliloquies, in presentational contracts, 55, 57
Songs, in presentational contracts, 55
Sophocles. See *Antigone* (Sophocles)
Spectacle, and stage effects, 7
Stage directions
character information and, 69
in *The Glass Menagerie*, 61
visualizing during the first reading, 13–14
Stanislavsky, Constantin, 7, 37, 84
Strindberg, August, 56
Supplemental research
biographical/autobiographical materials as, 88–89
for *Hamlet*, 123–125
Internet as source of, 92–93
interviews as source of, 89–90
literary criticism as source of, 91–92
original theatrical conditions as source of, 92
past productions as source of, 90–91
Synge, John Millington, 40
Synthesis
conflict analysis and, 5
of Shakespeare's *Hamlet*, 125
of *The Glass Menagerie*, 105–106

Tactics of characters, 68
Tartuffe (Molière)
blocking character in, 20
conflict analysis through actions and beats in, 85
denouement in, 28
dialogue revealing characters in, 17–18
given circumstances in, 44
major dramatic question in, 30
presentational theatrical contract in, 57
protagonist in, 26
relating the play's elements to conflict, 101–105
scene as a unit of conflict in, 79
simple vs. complex behavior in, 67
stage directions in, 69
synthesis of elements in, 100–105
tactical strategies of characters in, 68
theme related to conflict in, 100–101
Theatrical conditions, original, 92
Theatrical contract(s), 53–62
definition of, 53
general questions about, 62
in *Hamlet*, 118–120
nonrealistic. See Nonrealistic theater contracts
presentational and representational, 54
realistic, 54, 57
theatrical conventions vs., 54
in *The Glass Menagerie*, 60–61
Theme vs. conflict, 97–101
Thought process, 76, 120
Time frame, as part of given circumstances, 39–40, 45–46
Tragedies, essential structures of, 20
Translated plays, 43

Understanding August Wilson (Bogumil), 91

Williams, Tennessee. See *Glass Menagerie, The* (Williams)
Wilson, August, 13–15, 28, 44, 56, 69, 89
World of Tennessee Williams, The (Leavitt), 89

Year of the King, The: An Actor's Diary and Sketchbook (Sher), 88